I0165281

PERSONAL REVOLUTION

JOSHUA SPEARS

Copyright © 2018 Joshua Spears

All rights reserved. This book or parts thereof may not be reproduced in any form, stored in any retrieval system, or transmitted in any form by any means—electronic, mechanical, photocopy, recording, or otherwise—without prior written permission of the author, except as provided by United States of America copyright law. For permission requests, write to the author at the e-mail address below.

ISBN: 978-0-9600765-0-5 (Paperback)
ISBN: 978-0-9600765-1-2 (eBook)

Library of Congress Number: 2018914244

Book design, cover design, and edits by Alyssa Hodge

First edition 2019

joshuaspears@joshuaspears.com

www. joshuaspears.com

ACKNOWLEDGEMENTS

I wish to dedicate this book to the two most influential people in my life—my amazing wife, Julie, and my loving mother, Gloria. Without their continuous love and support, I would not be the man I am today.

Thank you to both of you for challenging me in all aspects of my life and encouraging me to live my dream and change the world one person at a time. I love you both to the moon and back!

TABLE OF CONTENTS

INTRODUCTION

I remember the feeling in my gut as I looked down at the scale that read 411 pounds. What a terrifying feeling it was to be completely out of control. It was my third year in college, and I was on the verge of getting kicked out of school for my poor grades. I was hiding my sorrows in a mountain of donuts and drowning them in a sea of chocolate milk. My self-esteem was so bad that I would often fantasize about swerving into oncoming traffic. I had gone to the doctor for my depression and was on various medications, but nothing helped. I would often wake up wishing I hadn't. I would lie in my bed and cry and just hope something would change. There was no light, no hope, no dream; there was just darkness. This pain was blinding; it moved through my whole being. It came out in how I spoke, thought, and lived. The only realistic option for me was to gather the nerve to take my own life. The only drawback to this solution was that I did not want to hurt my family any more than I already had.

Fast forward to a short time ago in a hospital room just a couple miles away: I was crying, not because I had hurt myself or because I was in so much pain but because of the pure joy I felt as my wife and I welcomed our third baby boy into the world. How did I go from being a complete mess and wishing it would all just end to cherishing each day and appreciating how good I have it?

It changed because I started a personal revolution.

When I was in grade school, a kid I had become friends with told me that his mom said he was no longer allowed to hang out with me at school. She said I was a bad influence on him. I was leading him down the wrong path, and I was having a negative influence on his behavior. During this season of my life, I had been expelled from five schools for bullying others as well as constantly being in trouble with the law. Looking back on it now, I would have to agree with this friend's mother; at the time, however, I had a shortage of friends, and this was a very painful thing for me to hear.

Several years later, after graduating from college and having just been promoted to a much better position within my company, I was on vacation in my hometown. I stopped at a local fast food restaurant for a shake on a hot summer day. This old friend of mine was working the drive-through window. I could not help but think about what his Mom had said when we were young. There was certainly nothing wrong with my old friend having such a position, but it was not what his dream was when he was young. How did we get from me being a negative influence on him and leading him down the wrong path to him serving me at the drive-through window?

I had a personal revolution while he had stayed his current course.

Right after the Christmas when I was nine, my mom moved us abruptly to the safe house. It was a home for battered families—a place for women to hide out from their abusive husbands. It was closely monitored by the police, and its location was not revealed to the women's families. At first, I thought the move was a temporary adventure, like the many times my mom had attempted to leave in the past; however, after being there a short time, my mom sat me down in our upstairs room to give me the news. She told me she was going to divorce my dad. I remember screaming at her in anger and informing her of how much I hated her. She said she had to show my brother, my sister, and I that this was not how people should treat their family. She told me how my dad was treated by his dad and that he was treating us the same way. She said it had to stop. While I was filled with rage at first, I then made my Mom a promise. At the age of nine, I made a vow to her that this behavior would end in my generation.

A short time ago, my wife met me at the door as I was returning home. She was visibly upset, and I was very concerned as she looked as if she had been crying. When I walked in the door, I asked my wife what was wrong. She very tentatively and nervously informed me that our two-year-old son had hit our brand-new, fifty-inch TV with a toy and had ruined it. I replied to her that it was just a TV. A few minutes later she came out to see me on the deck and saw that I was laughing. She asked me what was so funny about our son smashing the brand new TV, and it was in that moment, sitting on that deck by myself, that it had occurred to me that I had kept my promise I made to my mom many years ago. The vow was not a faint promise I made to her; it had become a life goal for me. That thought stopped me in my tracks, and I was so overcome with joy that I could not help but laugh. How did I come from generations of rage-filled men to being able to laugh about a smashed TV? These changes are just a few that have happened in my life because of personal revolutions.

CHAPTER ONE
What Is a Personal Revolution?

Revolution: a sudden, radical, or complete change [1]

When one thinks of a revolution, it is often in the sense of a race, gender, country, or people who had been previously bound becoming free. History is full of great examples of revolutions where an idea sparked a revolt that led to widespread change. A personal revolution would be a person going from being bound to being free—not from dictators or a corrupt government but from the tyranny of the lies that hold us captive. A personal revolution is the moment when you experience a significant and complete change in yourself. It starts with that *ah-ha* moment when you suddenly get it. Once you get it internally, your life's challenges become much more possible and even enjoyable. It ignites you with a passion to go after your adversity with a new energy. It is like when you are working on a puzzle and search and search for a missing piece, and right before you tear the puzzle apart and return it because it is missing a piece, you find that piece right in front of you. It is like looking all over the house for your sunglasses; you tear apart your car, ransack all your drawers, and rip the cushions off your couch to desperately look for the glasses. Then you pass a mirror and see them on the top of your head. The sunglasses have been there all along, but for some silly reason, you failed to notice the obvious.

We often get so distracted by the questions of life that we forget we most

1   "Definition of Revolution," Merriam-Webster. September 19, 2018. https://www.merriam-webster.com/dictionary/revolution.

likely have the answers; we just miss them for various reasons. A personal revolution is when we find what we have desperately been searching for, even if in many cases we are not certain what exactly it is that we are looking for.

It has been said that we all have life-changing moments anywhere from six to ten times in our lives. The moments that we realize something, learn something, or discover something that changes our lives forever are personal revolutions. They are the magical moments when we realize that we matter, recognize the value of other people, or for the first time see our future with hope and excitement. A personal revolution is the moment you see a fire truck speed past and say to yourself that is what you want to do or the moment you say something to someone and it hits you that your words can hurt this person. The moment you are sitting in class with your favorite teacher and it hits you that this is how you want to leave your mark on the world and the moment you realize that you create your world are both personal revolutions. A Personal Revolution is a revolution because it can change the trajectory of your life. It is personal because it changes you forever. Finding these moments is what Personal Revolution is all about. Your personal revolution is coming, and together we will start it.

MY FIRST PERSONAL REVOLUTION

I came up with the idea for personal revolution when I was twenty years old and in my third year of college. I found myself in misery and with no hope for the future. I had gone off to college with dreams of becoming a college football star, but my dreams were not my reality. I was having a terrible time dealing with my reality.

I had overcome so much but found myself in a dark place. I was on the verge of being kicked out of college for failing too many classes and losing any ability to get student loans for the same reason. I had feet injuries that prevented me from playing football anymore and had also lost all self-control with eating. I was well over 400 pounds and was in a constant state of despair. I had gone to my doctor about my weight as well as about my depression, but nothing seemed to make any difference. I had alienated myself from most of my friends for various reasons. Most of the issues with my friends revolved around imaginary offenses that I made up in my mind because of my low self-esteem. I had family that loved me, but I often looked at their attempts to help me as judgmental persecution instead of loving help. I grew up attending church but had watched several people who I looked up to as a youth make mistakes. I took their failure as a sign that all religion was a joke.

I had overcome so much and still found no answers and no peace. While the downhill spiral continued, I just hated myself, my life, and most of the world. My past victories made this situation even more hopeless because of the frustration that came from thinking that I should be better than this.

We all see personal revolutions around us that we may not think of as personal revolutions, but that is exactly what they are. Think of a person you know who used to be too heavy. This is something we can all relate to on some level, but we all know someone or have heard of someone who was big their whole life, and then just magically one day we see them after we haven't for a while and they have lost a ton of weight. This person, for whatever reason unique to them, got an understanding that they did not have before that led to their change. Maybe they went to the doctor and got some challenging news, or maybe they simply hit that tipping point where they wanted to change. But they made a significant change in their life that was not easy to do. This is a personal revolution.

Many of us know a person—sometimes an old uncle or maybe even just a friend—that was a smoker who one day was no longer a smoker. That is not to say it was easy or that it happened without effort or help. Along their path of life, they learned something or they had something happen to them that changed how they saw their situation. They had a personal revolution. The chains that bound them are now gone, and they are free. Personal revolutions can come in all shapes and sizes, but the one thing that is constant is that they make our lives better.

What we will be diving into in this book are some recurring themes to personal revolutions—things that we can think about and do that will compel us to make those changes.

One very interesting thing I have learned as I have shared my story with groups of all shapes and sizes is that my story is much more common than I previously thought. That is not to say that all people had my challenges; it is more to say that we all have challenges. We all have things about ourselves that we would like to change. This journey we take together will be about unpacking these issues. What we will find is that many of life's challenges have reoccurring themes. There are certain problems we all have that are unique to us, but in many cases they are the same problems. Personal Revolution is about seeking them out, exposing them, and working toward starting your personal revolution. Let the revolutions begin!

CHAPTER TWO
Sometimes the Answers Find You

My early years in college were that of a drifter. I did not have a specific plan for once I got to college, and it was showing in my performance. This lack of focus and direction was evidenced by the letter I got from the university informing me that my current semester was my final semester if I failed to raise the bar. The previous semester I had two classes I had simply quit going to and had just taken the failing grade in. I would often take classes just because they fell into a certain time slot. During this time of eating myself into oblivion, long hours of skipping class, and watching movies, I stumbled into an entry-level Communications 101 class that I took for no reason other than that it fit my schedule. This class, however, would be the start of my personal revolution. This class would change my life forever. You might be asking yourself what I could possibly learn in an entry-level class that could change my life so drastically; well, I'll tell you.

The class was about speaking or relating to people, but as mentioned before, to me it was just another class. The professor began to teach about Communication theory and different ways of relating to people. Early in the class, we began a section on perception. Perception is a word we have all heard and many of us often use. But for me, learning about perception as it related to my self-image was the beginning of the revolution.

I began to learn that my perception of myself, my life, and my family was all twisted. I had been walking through my life with the perception that everyone hated me and thought I was a loser. I had a twisted perception of myself as I felt that everyone was correct in this fictional assumption of me. At the time, this was a fact that I believed to be the truth. As I began to learn about this perception, what was the most eye-opening to me was the *why* behind it. Knowing why and how we develop these false perceptions is a key to us unlocking the door of this fictional prison. Our self-perception leads to our self-esteem.

Why did I see myself in this sick and twisted way? As babies, we all start as a blank slate; how did I get so twisted? What happened to me that I was so convinced that I was a certain way? My perception of myself had been destroyed as a young boy. My father played a very large role in the start of my negative self-perception, both with his constant, negative words and his actions toward me. I began to do some research about how he became the person he had become and learned that his father had treated him the same way. I also learned that my grandfather's father had treated my grandfather the same way. My self-image was further annihilated by bullies in school and teasing friends. But one of the key aspects of perception was when I learned that my father was broken himself. Once I learned that he was broken and that his thoughts, words, and actions had little to do with me and more to do with him being broken, I was then able to challenge his credibility to assess me. My perception of what I was told as a boy had been exposed as being from an unreliable source. This caused me to take inventory of all the aspects of my self-esteem that had been skewed by this unreliable source.

- -**ANSWER THESE QUESTIONS**

If you look back at your own childhood, you may find some similar skeletons in the closet. Maybe it was not a parent or a bully that made you feel *less than*, but we all have a story. Take a moment to look back and ask yourself these questions:

What is your perception of yourself?

_____

_____

Who helped you form that opinion of yourself?

_____

_____

Are they credible?

_____

_____

- -

If you are walking down a busy city street and a homeless man approaches you to try to sell you on an idea of how to make millions, you would look at the man and wonder what he could teach you about being rich when he lives on the street.

While that example is an oversimplified way of looking at this issue, the principle is true just the same. I had spent my life believing that what certain people said about me was fact, when in reality, these people had no clue what they were talking about. Once I learned that the statements they had made were nothing more than lies, I was able to reevaluate how I looked at myself. While I took the things they said as a proclamation of what I was, the reality is they were only projections of who those people were.

If you spend the entire first twenty years of your lifetime acting on a fact and then learn that this fact is actually a lie, then many of your thoughts and ideas will get blown apart. Like a young child who learns that Santa is not real, you look at Christmas differently once you know that a man in a sleigh is not delivering presents.

The first step for you and me as we start a personal revolution is to challenge the perception of ourselves. If we are honest with ourselves, we most likely will find that our perception is wrong. When this problem goes untreated, it can be like a sliver in your hand. It starts out small and eventually gets infected and grows into a seriously painful and swollen wound. Learning you are not what others say about you is like removing that sliver. Once the sliver is gone, you are not instantly healed, but at least the cause of the injury is gone, and the healing can begin.

Once you have challenged the perceptions you have had about yourself and learn that they may be unfounded, it is time to dig into fixing the broken self-perceptions that have created an unhealthy self-image.

TALKING TO YOURSELF

I had read many books on self-image and self-esteem in the past, but none of the ideas in these books stuck until one day in class, a professor used an example I could absolutely relate to. I have used this example countless times in front of thousands of people, as I feel it is a very simple and effective way to identify our self-esteem.

Have you ever noticed that when you are in your car on the way to a familiar destination, you rarely can remember the trip? You get in the car, buckle your seatbelt, adjust the radio, and pull out of the driveway, and then suddenly you are there. You observed all the traffic signs and made all the right turns, but you got there just kind of on auto pilot. Notice this about yourself; it happens every day.

What we often fail to notice is that during the entire trip, we are talking to ourselves —not out loud but in our own minds. We are playing a newsreel of our day ahead and our days behind. We are talking to ourselves about our family, friends, work, and any other things we have going on. It is almost like we are watching our life on the movie screen of our minds.

Are we a victorious conqueror who can do anything we want in life? If we have a new class coming up, are we pumped about learning new things and getting an A? If we are talking to ourselves about work, are we excited about a new promotional opportunity we have in the future? Some of us are this way, but many of us are not. Many of us talk to ourselves in a judgmental, negative way. We overanalyze our mistakes and failures, and they balloon into us knowing for a fact we will fail that class and never get that job. All of this happens without any consultation from anyone other than our own thoughts.

- -ANSWER THESE QUESITONS

When you talk to yourself, what are you saying?

_____

_____

What tone are you using?

_____

_____

Is there a positive or a negative theme?

_____

_____

- -

GLASS JUG

There is a story about an old pumpkin farmer. This old farmer was prone to go out in his field and just walk and think. During these walks he would often ponder life and just take in the beauty of his field. One day while walking through his field early in the season, he came across an old glass jug.

16

Just out of curiosity, he took the glass jug and put one of the baby pumpkins inside of it. He went on with his walk and thought little of it. As harvest time came, what used to be a field full of small, baby pumpkins was now a field full of large, full-grown pumpkins. As he was on his walk, he came across this glass jug. The pumpkin he had placed in the jug completely filled its glass prison. It had grown into every corner of the jug but was significantly smaller than the rest of the pumpkins in the field.

Our self-image is much like this glass jug. Holding a low opinion of ourselves is like putting ourselves in a glass prison. It is not possible for the baby pumpkin to grow bigger than the jug; our lives are much the same. If we hold limiting and destructive beliefs about ourselves, we are limiting ourselves before we ever get started. Where we differ from the baby pumpkin is we get to make a choice about our self-image. This choice will enhance or minimize our lives. The challenge to this is many of us don't know we are making that all-too-important choice.

SELF-IMAGE ASSASSINATION

Many of us have challenges growing up and people in our lives that are a negative force. Some of us eventually learn about self-esteem in school or in books; however, it seems to be rare that people learn about it as early as they would like to. Most of the people I talk to wish they had learned about self-esteem earlier on.

Our self-image begins forming when we are an infant. Some say it starts in the womb. It begins when our parents take care of our needs. Babies learn that by crying, they get what they want and need. As they grow up into toddlers and little children, they learn to talk and listen, and this furthers the path. They form a mental picture of themselves based on how they are treated. This same process continues in school and progresses until we are an adult. The simple way to view self-image is how we see ourselves.

Our parents play huge roles in our lives, and while I had a loving mother and many great family members who loved me, I had a father who destroyed my self-image. Each one of us has a story unique to us.

STUPID OL' JOSH

I remember living in fear of my dad when I was a young boy. He was a very volatile person. A few situations played out in my mind as I learned about why my self-image was so broken. My dad and uncles were all into radio-controlled cars when I was a boy. We had two cars and a little race-track set up in the garage. I would often watch them in wonder as they raced the trucks. Sometimes my dad would let me drive the cars, but most of the time I was a spectator. Often the cars would hit a pole or another car and a part on the front end would break. I had watched my dad several times when he glued the pieces back together.

One time while my dad was working, I drove the car. This was something that he had told me not to do. Just as I had many times before, I hit a pole and broke the front of the car. I had seen my dad fix it several times, so I thought I would give it a shot. Later on when my dad got home, he found the repaired radio-controlled truck that I had glued back together. But I had glued it so that the wheels would no longer turn. As you can imagine, my dad was very upset.

As a parent, on many levels I would agree that I was wrong to do what I did and should have been punished. But how my dad responded was not punishment in this case; it was a full-blown assault on my self-esteem.

My Grandparents from my mother's side of the family were coming down that day, and anytime I got to be around them was a treat for me. My grandparents were both loving and caring, and both of them were my heroes.

I remember that day like it was yesterday. My dad sat across from me, and my grandpa sat to my left. My dad was telling my grandpa about the radio-controlled truck, and he said, "stupid ol' Josh ruined the RC car." But the comments didn't end there. *Stupid ol' josh can't behave in school. Stupid ol' Josh can't get good grades.* I remember sitting there feeling absolutely terrible. I also remember the look on my grandfather's face; I could tell he was embarrassed. He just listened as my dad ran me down. What could he do? He tried to change the subject, but my dad just kept coming back to Stupid ol' Josh.. In my grandfather's shoes, I can understand why he did not correct my dad directly. My grandpa was at his son in-law's home and was courteous as a guest should be. With my dad's history of a hot temper, my grandfather was no doubt in a very difficult position. I knew my grandpa loved me, and I was humiliated that he was hearing these comments that made me feel like I was being trashed in front of my hero.

The hard part to hear was not the fact that I was constantly in trouble in school, that I ruined the RC car, or that I was a problem child. It was *stupid ol' Josh*. My dad did not address my behavior so much as he destroyed who I was. This was one of many instances when I learned how worthless I was, and that lie would stick with me for years. Does any of this ring a bell with you? On some level, I am sure it does.

When we are young, we are in the forming stages of our self-esteem, so many of us get broken at a young age. It takes years to recover if we ever do. From my experience in sharing my story and talking to others about their self-esteem challenges, this is the case over and over again. It is very common for audience members at my speaking engagements to come up to me and share stories that match and exceed mine in difficulty.

- **ANSWER THIS QUESTION**

Can you think of a situation in your past that assassinated your self-image?

_____

_____

- -

BULLIES

I grew up in a low-income and dysfunctional home and have always been heavy, so I was often teased for my status as well as for my weight. I can think of several instances where my self-image was murdered as a youth by my peers, but none stand out like the trip to the baseball field.

I was visiting my grandparents, and my grandpa and I were on our way back to his house. We drove past the baseball field near his house, and some kids were playing baseball. I asked my Grandpa if I could go play with them, and he said I could as long as I came home before dark. He lived half a mile from the field.

My grandpa dropped me off, and I walked down the right field line. I remember being very nervous about asking these kids if I could play because I was often not greeted kindly by my peers. I got to first base and asked the other kids whether they minded if I played with them.

"Get the hell out of here, fatso. You're not welcome here." The kids said a bunch of other mean things and let me know that if I didn't leave they would mess me up.

I was devastated and hurt by the rejection, and I walked back down the right field line with my head down feeling like stupid ol' Josh. Then I felt a tap on my shoulder. When I turned around—BAM—I got hit right in the face; it was the kind of hit that made me see stars. Next thing I knew, I was on the ground, and ten kids were pounding on me.

I walked home that day sobbing. My white shirt was completely covered in my own blood. As I walked home I remember thinking *stupid ol' Josh*. I should have known not to try to play baseball with those kids.. I learned at home that I was worthless, and it was confirmed by others. I went on believing these lies for many years.

For many of us, these assaults on our self-image are not so drastic or dramatic. They may come from not getting enough attention growing up, or at least not getting enough of the attention that we perceived we needed. It has been said the best thing a parent can do for a child's self-esteem is to listen to them. This teaches the child that what they say matters and thus what they think matters. This leads to children knowing they matter. Some of us had busy parents that were not abusive but maybe absent in the attention department.

Some people have bullies that terrorize them. This mean behavior is like a stone that is tossed into a smooth lake. Long after the stone has passed the surface of the water, the ripples of the wave go on and on. In some cases, these small waves grow larger and turn tragic.

Whether it is a parent, bully, sibling, or another person in our lives, we all have people who have affected how we see ourselves. It is human nature and goes with the territory of knowing people. As with the example of the pumpkin in the glass jug, we may have people in our lives that have convinced us that we are only to be a runt pumpkin. It is mandatory that we learn to interrogate these assumptions about ourselves. While others do impact us, they do not hold the key to our glass prison; we do.

- -ANSWER THESE QUESTIONS

Has anybody ever assaulted your self-esteem? Most people I meet and talk to have had their self-image attacked but have not yet had that *ah-ha* moment that allows them to pinpoint those attacks. On some level, we all experience these assaults. The challenge here is to identify them and realize where our perception of ourselves comes from.

What is your story? How do you see yourself?

_____

_____

Have you had situations in your life or people in your life that have destroyed how you see yourself?

_____

_____

When you talk to yourself, what are you saying?

_____

_____

Do you have your own version of a stupid ol' Josh story?

_____

_____

Think on that for a moment.
Well guess what, that's trash, and let's work on taking it out!

- -

CHAPTER THREE
Self-Image Restoration

The first step to working on your personal revolution and addressing your self-image journey is to take inventory of your current location. Have you ever spent the night in a hotel and noticed that on the back of your hotel room door there is often a map? The map usually says *in case of fire* on it. It is a map of the floor you are on and where the nearest fire exits are located. The first thing we would look for if we encounter an emergency is the location on the map that says *Fire Exit*; however, we would walk up and down the hall aimlessly and never find the fire escape unless we found the dot on the map that reads *you are here*. Without knowing where we currently are on the map the map is useless. So it goes with our self-image.

Until we ask ourselves the right questions to identify the current state of our self-image, we will never be able to fix it.

- -ANSWER THESE QUESTIONS

What are the right questions? As I mentioned in the example of riding in your car to work or school, think about when you talk to yourself; what are you saying?

When you think of what others think of you, do you see yourself in a positive way, or do you automatically feel as if they view you in a negative way?

Do you see yourself as a victim or victor in the battle of life?

_____

_____

Have you believed lies?

_____

_____

- -

STEPS TO IMPROVE YOUR SELF-IMAGE

Step 1: You Are Here!

Asking these questions and finding your own answers will help you find the *you are here* spot on your map. But once you have found that spot, you must come to the understanding that it is very possible that the information you have is incorrect. It is very possible that you have been holding a much too low opinion of yourself.

I was on my way to a speaking engagement recently, and I found myself not sure of where I was. I had recently gotten a new phone and was not familiar with the GPS function it had. I put in the address and started to try and find my way. After driving for some time, I began to realize that I could be going in the wrong direction.

I then looked at the map on the phone, and after looking at the compass in my car, it became clear why this fancy phone and GPS were leading me astray. I was taking roads that I thought were south that were really north and vice versa. The map function on the phone was unfamiliar to me, and I was operating under an understanding of direction that was flawed. So I was going further and further from my destination.

If we are living our lives on the understanding that we are a failure and destined for doom, we act accordingly. With all the people we meet and situations we find ourselves in, we act as if this direction is accurate. We often unintentionally sabotage ourselves. In our minds we have lost the race of life before the starting gun has even gone off.

Our ability to learn to know ourselves and understand that voice in our head is essential to starting a personal revolution. We are what we consistently think about ourselves. Knowing this and knowing that we control it is mandatory to having a personal revolution.

23

How is your GPS?

_____

_____

Is it accurate?

_____

_____

- -

Step 2: Forgive Others

If we look back on our childhood we will often find people in our lives that have hurt us in the past. While the way they treated us may have been wrong and destructive to us, what we often fail to realize is that by holding on to that, we are letting their destruction continue.

While we may feel that we are entitled to hold on to this justified anger or hurt, it is essential to view it as taking poison and waiting for the other person to die. The hurt, anger, rage, and pain we hold toward this person poisons us emotionally. While it is poisoning us, the other person is going on with their life and paying our anger no attention. It is as if they are living rent free in our heads.

It is not possible to follow the rest of the steps to a positive self-image while holding on to all of our past injuries. It may be hard to let things go, but we have to look at it as a surgery to remove a cancer. It hurts, and it may need to be done over time, but the key is we must learn to let it go. If we hold on to these past offenses, we keep reliving how someone hurt us in the past, so in our minds, this event happens over and over again. It takes a moment to grasp this, but while in our mind we think not forgiving others is hurting them, it is only we who suffer.

People often hurt us through their own inadequacies. They have their own problems and are often broken themselves. When I did the research about my dad and learned about his childhood, I learned that he was broken as a child himself. His dad mistreated him as his dad mistreated him, and the cycle was continued to me. So all the things he said to me were a result of him operating with a broken GPS himself. It clicked for me when I understood why he was so mixed up. It put his actions into perspective for me, and it became easy for me to let it go. I learned to love him for who he is rather than hate him for who he is not. In many ways I felt sorry for him. This occurred to me one day after not speaking to him for several years. When I realized that I had cracked the code with letting it go, I felt a massive, emotional weight lift off my chest.

If someone has hurt us or continues to do so, they are saying more about themselves than they are about us. Their information is incorrect, so when we learn that what they say or do to us has little do with us and more to do with them, we are free to let it go. This can be a difficult process for us to go through, but for our own sake, we must go through it. The past will still have happened, but how we look at it will shape our own future.

If we focus on the negative things people do to us, our focus toward ourselves will naturally veer toward the negative. It is like doing a word search; you keep looking for letters that make up words, and after doing this for a while, you try reading. While reading, you will keep noticing words within words. We train ourselves to look at letters a certain way, just like we do with others. When we focus on what they did to us and how messed up they are, we cannot help but look at ourselves in the same way. How you see other people shapes how you see yourself; forgiving them allows you to see yourself with that same forgiving lens.

Step 3: Forgive Yourself

We are often decent at letting the wrongs of others go, but when it comes to letting ourselves off the hook, we can't. We have all made stupid mistakes. We have been at parties and said stupid things that later on made us feel or look like a fool. We have all had relationships that we ruined by being an idiot. What we often fail to realize is that everybody has.

When we are struggling with a low self-image, we often magnify our flaws and minimize our good qualities. One of the key ways we do this is by focusing on and reliving the past.

When I had my personal revolution and was able to look back at my youth as an adult, I was very ashamed of several things. I remember all the people I mistreated. I thought of all the kids that I had bullied. I have a cousin who is my little sister's age. She used to come over all the time and play with my sister. I often teased her, made fun of her, locked her in closets, and did many mean, big-brother things to her. As an adult, every time I saw a post from her on social media, I felt guilty about the entire trauma I had caused her. This guilt often ruined my morning because it led to me thinking about all the other people I mistreated.

One day I decided to send her a message and apologize for all my past actions and ask for her forgiveness. I was shocked to find out that she had totally let it go and was able to laugh about it now. That is not to say that all of our past mistakes are laughable; however, I was torturing myself over ruining this person's childhood and that simply was not the case. My low self-esteem cornered me into seeing myself as this super villain in her life and this was not true.

---------------------------------**ANSWER THESE QUESTIONS**

Are there people in your life that you have wronged and you are beating yourself up over it?

_____

_____

Who is it? What did you do?

_____

_____

I challenge you to stop for a moment and think about that question.

Once you get a couple of people in your mind, reach out to them and ask for their forgiveness. Depending on what you did to them, you may find that while you are beating yourself up over it, they have moved on. In some cases, they may choose to hold on to their anger. If that is the case, you must still make the decision to forgive yourself. The past is long gone, and holding on to this regret will needlessly torture you.

Holding on to the hurt others have caused us is a cancer, and so is holding on to our own past mistakes. We need to be able to allow ourselves to be human and accept our mistakes as what they were—mistakes. It is hard not to act human when you are one.

----------------------------------**ANSWER THIS QUESTION**

Think about a person in your life that you love dearly—this may be a little brother, a sister, or a friend—who has had some problems and is a person in your life that you have been an anchor for. They come to you when they need help or a lift. We all have a few; take a few moments and think of your person.

Who is this person?

_____

_____

Now imagine the thing that is bothering you that you did to someone else. Imagine that the person you help all the time made the same mistake. How do you view them? I bet you view them in a much kinder and softer way than you view yourself. You forgive them; you understand that they are human and make mistakes. You understand they are still learning. You get that they don't have all the answers. We can often let people off for their crimes with probation while we give ourselves life in prison. We must use our key and open the cell door.

- -

Step 4: See Yourself at Your Best

We often think that if we hold a low opinion of ourselves, it is some self-less, virtuous act. We see someone who is arrogant and think that person is a jerk. That person may be a jerk, but doing the total opposite of that person is a mistake.

This misunderstanding of holding a low opinion of ourselves has ruined many lives. This misunderstanding is a lie that leads to misery.

Some of us have a difficult time seeing ourselves at our best. Sometimes we need to do an intentional exercise to help get the process going. I remember when it hit me that I had bought into these lies.

I was in college and had recently started my personal revolution. When I started, I was over 400 lbs. and in the depths of depression on a daily basis. I started the Revolution and started to lose weight and feel happier. I went home for the weekend and was at a family gathering with many of my aunts and uncles. We were all at my grandparents' house, and I was alone in the living room with several of my family members. I had always thought I knew how they viewed me, but what I found out was so liberating.

They began to ask me how I was doing, and they all seemed to notice the change in me without me telling them directly. So I decided to share my personal revolution with them, and they wanted to hear more. I began to tell each of them how I thought they viewed me. I told my oldest aunt that I thought she saw me as a total trouble maker and someone she was embarrassed to tell people she was related to. She rode me all the time about my troubles in school. She was always telling me I needed to shape up, so I thought she must hate me. She told me that was crazy and that she was proud of me. She rode me because she cared about me and knew I could do great things. I had thought another aunt of mine viewed me as a scuzzy person that was no good. She had young kids, and I always thought that she thought I was a bad influence on her kids. She started laughing at me and asked me whether I thought she would have had me babysit all the time for her boys if she thought I was a bad influence. Then came an uncle who I worked for in the summers. I thought he thought I was lazy and a bad worker and that I was a charity case that he was helping because he felt guilty. The look on his face was amazement, and he said I was one of the best people he had ever had work for him.

All of these people have known me since I was born. They had witnessed the ups and downs of my life and knew me well. In my mind, they all looked down on me with disappointment and disgust. My statements of how I thought they viewed me were so far off that they almost thought I was joking. I think it is a safe bet the same would be true for you.

When each of them told me how proud they were of me and that the reason they were driving me so hard was because they loved me, I was blown away. I thought they did not want me around their kids when in fact they were telling their kids to be more like me; it was jaw-dropping.

- **ANSWER THIS QUESTION**

Who in your life can you seek out to help expose the lies you have believed for years?

_____

_____

Think of these people and go to them and share with them how you think they see you. I bet you will find the same thing that I did.

- -

One of the keys to seeing yourself at your best is to come to the understanding that you have bought in to a bunch of lies. You need to expose them for the trash they are and take them out accordingly.

Another huge aspect to how we need to work on seeing ourselves at our best is examining how we talk about ourselves. After making a stupid mistake, how many of us would say to ourselves *I am such an idiot* or *I am so stupid?* We do this almost as second nature; we don't think too much of it. What we need to realize is that by making these statements, we are fueling the wrong fire.

I had a teacher in the sixth grade who told me something all the time, but it took me years to understand how right he was. I had been kicked out of several schools before, and before I could even start at his school, my mom and I had to meet with him to discuss whether they would take me in this school. It was a Christian school that had the right to not allow me in. The teacher told my mom he was up for the challenge and allowed me to enter his class.

Over the course of a short period of time, I began to screw up in his class. Then one day he sat me down while the other kids were on a break. He began to point out to me that I always ran myself down and that he was no longer going to tolerate it. This blew me away, so I asked for clarification.

I would often say I was such an idiot or such a loser. He told me that, going forward, anytime I made comments like this, I would have to write sentences. The sentences were always different, but each time they had the same effect of building nature. For instance, I might have had to write, "I am a unique person who has tons of potential" or "I can do all things through Christ who strengthens me". Since it was a Christian school, the sentences I had to write were often scriptures. As with most experiences I had with people who tried to help me, I didn't quite get the point of the exercise at the time, but it was still effective.

It took me years to understand fully how right this teacher was, but the point is timeless. If we always talk about ourselves in a negative way, we cannot possibly see ourselves at our best. Our words are a verbal manifestation of our thoughts; we build our thoughts further by giving them the light of our words. So when we speak our negative thoughts about ourselves, we help those thoughts grow.

How about you? How do you talk about yourself?

_____

_____

- -

If you're like I was—and still am at times—you often run yourself down. Try talking about yourself like you would talk about your friend—in a positive building way. It won't take long, and you will really start to believe what you are saying.

Each day we are all confronted with thousands of choices from what shirt to wear to what route to take to work. The biggest and most influential choice we make every day is how we *choose* to see and speak about ourselves. This choice impacts so many others.

Step 6: Build Other People Up

Building other people up is one of the key aspects to building a positive self-image. It is almost impossible to feel bad about yourself when you are serving someone else.

I recently went to visit an organization that helps special-needs students. It is an amazing place designed to help these students become more functional in society. It had a total mock-up of a town with a bank, stores, traffic lights, and so on. The special-needs kids come there with their school or even after school to learn life skills. One of the most amazing things about my tour was when the director told me that every person working there was a volunteer. Many of the volunteers were retirees and so forth, but what blew my mind was the number of teens. The organization has 400 teen volunteers and a large waiting list of people who want to volunteer. I asked the director what drives the strong desire to volunteer, especially from young people? She told me that the young people who served there left feeling good and encouraged themselves.

As I left, the experience I had there reminded me of this key to a positive self-image. These people give freely of their time to help others that are less fortunate. While they are wrapped up in helping others, they lose themselves in the great work they are doing. They are not only thinking about the needs of others but also witnessing the good they are currently doing. While watching and thinking about the great things we do in the lives of others, it is natural that we begin to view ourselves with kinder eyes.

When we think about our mind and thoughts, another way to increase positive thinking is to ask whether we have windows or mirrors. If we have mirrors, we are always looking at the world as it relates to us. We are thinking about how we look, what we have going on, and what is good for us. If we are in a constant state of looking at ourselves, we often start to pick ourselves apart. If we turn the mirrors of our mind into windows, we start to see what other people have to offer and how we can help them. This practice minimizes our own issues.

How about you? Who do you have in your life that you can help? Maybe it is the person who sits next to you in homeroom or the person who has the cubicle next to you. Is there a nearby organization that you could join in order to help people?

I am not suggesting that we forget our own issues and bury them with acts of kindness toward others. A better description of this would be that many of our self-esteem issues are from overthinking and overanalyzing. Most of our self-image issues are fiction. Since they are fiction, they should be forgotten about. If we constantly think about us and what we have going on, we will not be able to grow.

A great by-product of focusing on helping others by building them up is they will naturally build us up more. Because we get what we put into relationships, the more we invest in others, the more they invest in us.

- -ANSWER THESE QUESTIONS

In what areas could you serve others more?

_____

_____

Who could you be serving, and when could you start?

_____

_____

- -

SELF-ESTEEM CONCLUSION

The single most important thing that drives your personal revolution is going to be your self-image. If you see yourself as a broken and miserable person, then you will not be able to move on to any of the next steps. Your self-image is how you see you. What many of us forget is that we create our self-images daily with how we talk to ourselves in our own minds. We need to learn to monitor these thoughts and take out the trash.

Be honest with yourself; think about the following statements and ask yourself whether these are things you say to yourself:

"I'm an idiot."

"I can't do it."

"They hate me."

"I give up."

"It's great they are doing so well, but I could never do that."

"These ideas work for other people, but they could never work for me."

These statements are as much trash as a used-up milk carton and need to be disposed of accordingly. Once we learn that we have the power to build our self-image, we can begin to see ourselves as the unique and amazing people we are. Remember that any significant revolution we have in our lives will come from the inside out. The first change we need to make internally is to challenge our self-image, expose the lies, and rebuild it.

1. You are here: Take inventory of the current state of your self-esteem.
2. Forgive others: Let go of the offenses of others; this gives us the power to move on.
3. Forgive yourself: Stop beating yourself up for mistakes you made in the past.
4. See yourself at your best: Choose to view yourself with kind eyes.
5. Watch what you say: Your words have the power to build or destroy.
6. Build other people up: Help others builds ourselves.

CHAPTER FOUR
Attitude

It has been said that attitude is the one thing that comes closest to being the only thing that determines our success and happiness. Two people start the same job at the same company on the same day. They work at the same location, have the same commute, and share the same direct supervisor. How is it that after ten years, one loves their job and the other hates it? The difference is their attitudes.

Once we have begun to see ourselves differently, we will notice things around us change drastically. Imagine you are walking down the sidewalk with a friend of yours. You are noticing all the cars going by, the green grass, and all the people you are encountering. You are bummed out and annoyed by the overcast day and wishing for sunlight. As you mention to your friend that you wish this overcast weather would go away so that you could get some sun, your friend looks at you in shock and says that you need to take off your sunglasses. You remove your sunglasses and notice it is bright and sunny. Your perception of what was going on around you was adjusted by the lenses of the glasses. These glasses are much like your attitude. Your attitude is the lens through which you see the world. This lens has a direct impact on everything you see and puts its own tint on things.

Our attitude is something that we often do not realize we have the power to control. Our attitudes, much like our self-images, are something we often go without checking. If you were brutalized as a youth by bullies or negative people who destroyed your perception of yourself, then it is safe to say that they also made an impact on your perception of your world. Since your attitude is your perception of the world around you, it is safe to say that a poor self-image and a poor attitude go hand-in-hand. How can you look at yourself with a twisted lens and then look at the world and see hope and possibility? The fact is that you can't. When you are starting a personal revolution and you begin to see yourself differently, you will be blown away by the attitude adjustment that follows.

ATTITUDE ADJUSTMENT

I was often told as a troubled youth that I needed an attitude adjustment. I never quite understood what people meant by that until I actually had one. I remember one of my first and most impactful attitude adjustments. This adjustment helped me drive significant change in my life.

I was going into the seventh grade, and it was the first day of school. I had gotten kicked out of two schools in the sixth grade and three others in the years before. I was on my way to an alternative school. I had been sent to this same school in the fifth grade, and my mom had pulled me out because she felt that her son was not like those other kids at the school. My mom was the type of mother that was always going up to the school and defending me and fighting for me. I would have problems in school, and she would go up to the school and talk to the teachers and administration and explain to them that the kids were picking on me or that the teachers were out to get me. This is a natural response of any parent who has a child that is struggling. The natural mother-bear mentality is to go after those who are hurting their child. In many cases, maybe the kids were picking on me, but the other kids or teachers would often be her focus instead of what I was doing. In her mind, I was justified in my behavior.

The behavior that got me kicked out of the various schools I attended was all over the map. Sometimes I would scream at the teachers, and other times I would assault my peers. I remember one of the last straws for me in one of the schools. I was going into classroom, and a student was in my seat. I asked him to move, but he would not. I grabbed him by the back of the head and slammed his head on the desk and then whipped him to the ground. This was senseless violence that was completely unprovoked, and there could be no excuse to justify it. This action led to me being expelled from my fifth school and would be my last day in a public school for several years.

Until one day when I was in the seventh grade, my mother always seemed to spin the situation so that it was not all my fault. I remember riding in the car that day on the way to the alternative school I was sent to. We had small, white car with a blue interior, and the ride was about thirty minutes. As we got near the school, my mom changed her tune with me. She said that she loved me but that she was not going to bail me out anymore. If someone was going to do something to me and I did something back, I was going to be responsible for what I did. I had put myself in that school and only I could get myself out. If a teacher asked me to do something and I wouldn't do it, then I would be responsible. If I got in trouble and was disciplined, then I would take that discipline and not argue with the teacher. Again my mom said she loved me, but she was not going to bail me out anymore because I created this situation and only I could fix it.

I got out of the car that day totally rejected and heartbroken. The one person who had defended me and helped me through all of these issues had thrown me to the curb. How could she have done that to me?

It was then for the first time that a sobering thought occurred to me. I thought, *is it possible that I am the problem?* Was it possible that I had truly created this mess for myself? Was it possible that the teachers were not out to get me?

I was operating with the attitude that everyone else was wrong and that everyone else had the problem. I never looked at myself. The attitude adjustment was painful, but it was a key moment for me to take ownership of my life. I am sure it was difficult and painful for my mom to cut me loose, but it had to be done. She would later share with me that this talk was something she had thought about for a long time. She told me that she had to prepare for it and pray for the courage to do it. She also told me that she cried all the way home. It was not the easy road, but it was the only road that would lead to my change. A personal revolution is often made up of several attitude adjustments, and in many cases, they do not feel good at the time.

To say this was the only attitude adjustment I had in my journey is not accurate. The fact is we often have to give ourselves attitude adjustments. The frustrating part is at times we have to re-adjust. Sometimes we need to be reminded as much as we need to be educated.

A FEW KEYS TO UNLOCK THE CHAINS OF A BAD ATTITUDE

Key 1: Learn to Monitor Your Attitude

There are often times when life will knock us down and wake us up to the negative attitude we have. I already told you about one of mine, what about you? Can you think of a time when your world got rocked and you learned you were looking at things all wrong? If you are honest with yourself, you will be able to find several instances.

While this does happen, the truth is most of the time there are subtle adjustments we must make. For example, you may at one point encounter a new program at work or school. Often our first reaction may be negative. We may see all the things wrong with the new program or routine. This is a somewhat normal reaction to change; however, we must ask ourselves a few questions if we feel the need to complain about it. If the first thing you think of when you hear of this new project or routine are all the things wrong with it, your attitude is limiting your ability to embrace change. Once we realize that our initial reaction to change is often negative, we begin to search for the benefits of the change. This is not to say that every change is good; sometimes changes are not. At times we must go back to the old way, but we will never know if something new will work unless we are willing to dive in all the way and give the change all we have. They key is to be aware of our own reaction to these situations. By being aware of our internal reaction, we can then challenge our initial assumptions about the change. This is a subtle yet effective attitude adjustment. A personal revolution is often started with a significant attitude adjustment, but for it to be sustained it must be followed up by consistent, subtle adjustments.

Key 2: Realize Your Attitude has Real Consequences

Many times people think about attitude like it is something vaguely out there that does not have any real-world impact. Nothing could be further from the truth. In my example at the beginning of the chapter, it was very obvious that the lens through which I saw the world was destroying my world. Many times the answer is not so obvious. One real-life example would be a new person in your life. Just for the sake of the example, let's say this person is a new in-law. Maybe your brother brings home a new woman and you initially don't like her. Your attitude toward her is that you see all the things you don't like about her. In your view, she is not a good fit for your brother. Follow this path through to its conclusion. As time goes by, they get married, and you are still sitting back and wondering what your brother is doing and what he sees in her. As time goes by, when she makes innocent remarks, you view them as shots at you and your family. Before you know it, this subtle, negative attitude toward her has turned into full-blown hatred.

The next thing you know, you want to scream anytime you look at her.

What if you had started off with the opposite attitude toward her? When you meet her, you check your attitude at the door. You make a commitment to yourself to try to see the best side of her. Soon you begin to learn that she is a lot like you. After a short period of time, you begin having conversations with her about life and learn that she is an amazing person. When the wedding comes, you are so excited for your brother and his new bride. Soon, their kids come and play with yours as you sit over coffee and converse with someone who is now one of your best friends.

Granted, this example is very cut and dry, and when dealing with people, things are never cut and dry. But the idea is that your attitude toward people impacts how you see them. This then impacts how you act toward them and leads to how they act toward you. So many times, monitoring our attitude produces real fruit; we can trade a mortal enemy for a lifetime friend all because we choose to monitor our attitude.

Key 3: Realize Your Attitude is Your Responsibility

I remember once when I was in college and working for my grandpa and uncle. They build and sell docks on the lake. I had had many jobs before working for them, but none of those jobs had worked out so well. I would often get mouthy with my boss or take offense to the direction people would give me. As with school, in the workplace this does not work. People become a liability when they can't be taught. One day after I did something wrong at work, my grandpa started to give me what I felt was a hard time about it. I started to complain. I started to talk about how this wasn't fair and that wasn't fair. I said I should be making more money. He came over to me and in a very firm manner put his hand on my shoulder. He said very loudly in my face that I had a big chip on my shoulder and that I needed to take it off. He then said that I needed to learn how to keep a boss happy no matter who that person was. I stormed off by myself; I was devastated. I remember feeling worthless and like I should quit.

I sat alone for a little bit and felt sorry for myself. Then the realization started to come to me. I realized, much like I did when I was a poor student, that I was the problem. I thought about what my grandpa told me and how much I pushed him before he finally gave it to me straight. I thought to myself that he would only do that if he felt like he had to. I made up my mind right then and there that I was going to blow everyone away with what a good worker I could be. If my grandpa and uncle wanted ten docks by lunch, then I was going to give them fifteen. I was going to prove to them and myself that I could do it. I am not saying I was the best worker ever; however, I will say that each summer after that, I got significant financial incentives from my grandpa to come back home and work for the summer. Before long, I was leading a crew. This resulted in my own little dock installation business that was my source of income the rest of the way through college.

I had the opportunity to either blame others and complain or own my attitude and my situation, and I made my choice. Much like the line *you can lead a horse to the water but you can't make him drink*, people will give us clues along the way, but unless we decide to take ownership of our attitude, we are like the thirsty horse standing next to the stream. How about you? Right now, what things in your life could you look at from a different perspective and change the entire situation for the better. If you don't have something, keep looking. It's there; we all have these situations. A personal revolution is had by seeking that situation out and demanding of yourself to make that change.

Key 4: Realize Your Attitude can Make You Happy or Miserable

I recently had a chance to spend some time with a sixty-five year old man who went through the painful process of watching his two daughters lose their lives to cancer. One was thirty-nine, and the other was forty-one. They passed away nine months apart. There are not words to describe the pain this situation caused this man and his family. His attitude toward the whole thing made it very clear to me that our attitude can make us happy or miserable, and it is our choice.

As he was telling me about the ups and downs of the battles they fought together as a family, I was thinking to myself that I would be out of my mind if this happened to me. As he spoke, I just listened, and he shared how much he loved his daughters and how happy he was with his grandkids. He shared with me how good he felt as a parent knowing how happy his daughters had been until they had cancer and how proud he was of them as they fought this devastating battle with strength and courage. His attitude was to see all the good things about the situation. The bad things about their passing were there and real, but he focused on the good things.

He could have caved into the obvious temptation to feel sorry for himself and complain about all that he had lost. He could have been very depressed as he spoke of his daughters knowing they had passed on. He could have thought of the grandkids and how their mother was gone, and he could have allowed fear and dread to overtake him. But that was not the choice he made.

He could have spent the rest of his years broken and bitter and mad at the world about the loss of his little girls. If anyone met him and knew what he had been through, they would say he was justified to be miserable because of it. The other option, the one he chose, is to stay positive and be thankful for the time he did have. Think about how much richer and fuller his life is because of his amazing daughters. The simple fact is this situation was not fair, not easy, and not ideal in any way. But his choice to look at it from one perspective instead of the other is the difference between him enjoying his life and hating it. Not many of us are confronted with this type of hurdle that could prevent us from having a positive outlook. But at times we often make the wrong choice. Think about the problems in your life right now. I am sure if you are honest, you will find that in most cases, what this man went through could be viewed as far worse than the challenges you have. If he can make his choice to remain positive in his circumstances, then we can use his example to make that same choice, regardless of our challenges. His choice to have this attitude amid such tragedy was no doubt a challenge, but he understands the value of that choice. Choose your attitude, and choose it wisely.

There are many things in all of our lives that are out of our control. Challenges and adversity will come to all of us at some point and on some level. We have the ability and power to shape our view of our world to our liking. It will reflect back to us how we see and act toward the world. No matter how bad we are treated by others or how disadvantaged we are, the fact remains that our attitude is one thing we can control and are responsible for. To some, this statement is painful because it means that we are a part of our own problems; however, this also means we are our own solutions. A personal revolution is about gaining freedom where we were once bound. Much like with our self-esteem, we are our own jailer, and we hold the key to our cell in our own hands. Unlock the cage!

– – – – – – – – – – – –KEYS TO UNLOCK THE CHAINS OF A BAD ATTITUDE

1. Learn to monitor your attitude.
2. Realize your attitude has real consequences.
3. Realize your attitude is your responsibility.
4. Realize your attitude can make you happy or miserable.

CHAPTER FIVE
Steps to Building a Good Attitude

I n the previous chapter, we identified clearly the role that attitude plays in our lives. Now we will look at how to build and maintain a good attitude. Our attitude is much like a plant; if you want to build a flowerbed, you must learn how to take care of a plant. The plant needs good soil, sunlight, water, and room to grow.

Step 1: Prepare the Soil

If you want to put in new flowers, the first thing you have to do is get the soil ready. There is more to it than just going to the hardware store and buying some topsoil. To prepare the soil, you must also remove all the leaves and debris from the soil. This is not a gardening book, but the metaphor is very accurate.

Much like we prepare the soil for the plant, if we want to build a good attitude, we must till the soil and remove all the weeds that are in the way. The negative perceptions we have about ourselves and others is just one type of weed. We must pluck these perceptions out of the soil and remove them down to the root. If you are still holding onto negative feelings toward other people, you may be nice to them, but you still haven't let it go in your heart. This is much like trimming the top of the weeds but leaving the roots in the soil. For a time they will not be visible, but they are still there, and with time they will return. These weeds will choke the good attitude plant you are working on. The energy needed from the soil to foster a good attitude will be silently robbed by these weeds. Not only will the new flower not grow but also will the weed soon emerge from the soil with a vengeance. This will lead to frustration because now to get rid of the weeds, you have to dig up the dirt and may damage the flower you just planted.

How is your soil? Is it clean? Purge your mind and heart of things that will keep you negative. Forgive the people that have offended you and forgive yourself for all the mistakes you are holding over your own head. Take them out of the garden, place them in a trashcan nearby, and let it go.

Step 2: Add Sunlight

The next thing a good plant needs to grow is sunlight. If we want to grow, we have to expose ourselves to light. Much like the weeds are people who have offended us in the past, a lack of light may mean that we are allowing people now to have a negative impact on us. Someone who is always negative, complaining, and never sees the good in life is much like placing an umbrella over our plant. We need to remove the negative obstacles and let the awesome light get to our plants. If you have a houseplant, you may have to move it closer to the window sometimes to increase the amount of light it gets. Maybe we need to move our personal plant some. At times we need to meet new people—people who are positive, encouraging, and uplifting—who will shine light down on our plants . Not long after we cut out the negative influences and embrace the positive ones, we begin to feel the sunlight as energy surging through our lives.

Step 3: Water the Seed

Everybody knows that plants need water to grow. Sometimes it rains, but in many cases we must take the time to water the plants ourselves. In our metaphor, water would be good ideas, good books, and positive situations. We may run into a few people across our path that can be like the rain that helps our plant grow, but in most situations we must be more strategic if we are going to feed our plant the water it needs, like good books, blogs, podcasts, and people. We must be strategic and sometimes go out of our way to ensure our plant is getting the water it needs to grow. Reading good books is a surefire way to inject yourself with the positive energy needed to grow. Trading a few comedy podcast for some good life-lesson type podcasts can change your whole perspective. You reap what you sow, and the same is true of what you put in your mind. It may rain, but people who have nice gardens know they must go out of their way to ensure their plants get the water they need.

I once heard a line once that really fits this plant metaphor: "Sometimes you can't see how big a plant can get until you put it in a bigger pot."

This is perfect; how often is our attitude limited by the low expectations we place on ourselves? We think we are too small, too slow, or too weak to be a certain way. Often we get to a point in our lives where our low expectations of ourselves are like a pot that used to be comfortable but is now choking our progress. A new pot may mean finding a new job or new friends but will almost always involve setting some new goals that are bigger and harder than we thought possible when we started. Until we get the bigger pot, we are hindering ourselves.

Step 5: Own your Garden

Our attitude is something we must manage daily, just like our garden of plants in our metaphor. We must know what trash is and take it out. We must strategically put good things into our minds and not limit ourselves with old thinking. But the thing we must take away from this is that we own our garden from start to finish. No matter what has been done to you, you own your attitude; no matter what anyone said to you, you own your attitude.

As with the garden, one thing is certain with our attitude; something will grow. Your garden will produce what you allow it to produce. If you fail to check and monitor your garden, you will reap a harvest of weeds. If you are strategic and act with purpose, you will get the attitude garden you are looking for.

Our attitude is the lens through which we see the world, but it is also a living organism, like a plant. It requires work to keep it up, and it takes someone owning it to ensure its survival.

KEYS TO MANAGING YOUR ATTITUDE

Treat your attitude like a bank account. Check it daily and ensure the balance is going in the right direction. If the balance is getting low, you need to make a deposit. The best way to ensure you like what you see when you check your attitude daily is to develop routines and make them mandatory.

In the back of this book is a list of some other great books to get you started. Reading every day has transformed my life. Develop a routine that is non-negotiable and makes positive deposits mandatory. Maybe for you, the right routine is getting up half of an hour earlier to read a powerful book. Having your morning coffee with a book instead of a screen in front of your face can change your life. But maybe this won't work for you; maybe you are a night owl. Swap the nightly screen time for a good book. Closing your day with a book instead of social media can change your life. If you are thinking that you hate to read, then I have to say that I am right there with you sometimes. But what about your commute to work or school? Jump in the car and fire up a good, uplifting podcast. There are thousands of them out there. Instead of letting your mind ponder all the challenges of your day, feed it with some good, positive energy. You will no doubt find that when you get to work you will feel more empowered and positive for the day than if you had spent the morning yakking on the phone about a football game.

This section is not an attack on devices, social media, talking on the phone, or football; these are just a few examples of ways that you can strategically attack a bad attitude. Each one of us may take a different route, but one thing is clear. We are responsible for our attitude. Our attitude will return to us exactly what we put into it. Having a personal revolution is about challenging our attitude and embracing the privilege of shaping it to fit our liking.

— — — — — — — — — — — — -STEPS TO CULTIVATE A POSITIVE ATTITUDE GARDEN

1. Prepare the soil: Remove the weeds of the negative thoughts choking your plants.
2. Add sunlight: Surround yourself with positive and uplifting people.
3. Water the seed: Strategically fill your mind with positive things.
4. Allow room to grow: Have high expectations for yourself and your attitude.
5. Own the garden: Something will grow; take ownership of it to get the attitude you want.

CHAPTER SIX
The People in Our Lives by Chance

The role of other people in our personal revolution is massive. It is not something that can be taken lightly. Nobody changes their lives by themselves. Whether we think so or not, people are always influencing us. Over the next two chapters we will unpack the different roles people play in our lives. We will look at people who we have little to no control over having in our lives, and then we will dive into people we do have control over having in our lives.

It is essential to think hard on the previous topics in this book thus far. We must learn to see ourselves in a positive and productive way before we can utilize the people around us. After having made this transformation, you begin to see your world with new eyes. You start to see the wonder of the world around you rather than all the challenges. Once you have started taking these steps, one of the most amazing things you will find is all the great people out there. Along the way you will also find that some of the people in your life you thought had one role actually have another role. For example, you may find friends that you thought were helping you are actually holding you back. In other cases you will find people you were certain were your enemies to be your best allies. Once you change, the view of your influences changes, and the roles people play in your life become clearer.

Sixty-five percent of Nobel Peace prize winners had a mentor who had previously won the award. It seems that the people who have won this very difficult award were not able to do it by themselves. While making significant life changes is not winning the Nobel Peace Prize, the principal is just the same. The people you are around and in the proximity of make a significant impact on your life.

In many ways our lives are like a blank canvas. Each person we meet takes their brush and makes a few strokes on our canvas. Some paint amazingly beautiful stokes, while others swing at it with a razor blade. When we are younger, our level of control over what people say or do to us is somewhat limited; however, when we grow up we have increasingly more control. The key to us allowing others to impact us in the most positive way is for us to decide what we want our finished painting to look like. If we know we want our painting to look a certain way, we then learn to seek out the type of people that are going to paint the correct types of strokes. If we never have a vision of what we want it to look like, we give all the power to other people to determine how our canvas of life turns out.

As we look back on our life canvases, it is easy to determine who was deliberately making good strokes, and who was just hacking away at it. As I look back at my canvas from when I was growing up, I had many negative influences that made the painting look like something a preschool student would bring home. With that being said, I did have many people who worked to turn those negative strokes into amazing art.

While my examples take us down this trail, it is important for you to analyze your own canvas. These examples are my story, but the idea is that no matter where you are or what you are going through, you can find people to help you start a revolution.

SCHOOL AND WORK INFLUENCES

Through my school years, up until the seventh grade, I viewed my teachers and other school staff as haters. They always seemed to be picking on me and running me into the ground. I felt in my heart that they were not looking out for me. I spent the majority of my middle school years in an alternative school. This school was filled with emotionally impaired students much like myself. I was surrounded by people with problems, and it was fitting because I had problems. While I was surrounded by many negative influences, there were several people who could see a better picture on my canvas.

Whether you are in school or the workplace, if you look at your situation the right way, there is no doubt you will see that you have people in your life right now that are just waiting to help you with your canvas.

I had a teacher in middle school who saw a masterpiece in me that I could not see at the time. Mr. Lee[2] was my gym teacher at the alternative school that I went to, and for whatever reason, he kept telling me I could change and do something with my life. Our relationship was deepened by our common love of sports. While Mr. Lee was a teacher at this school, he was also the junior varsity baseball coach for the local public high school. Mr. Lee was always willing to go to the next level to help me. One day in gym class, he came up with a plan to allow me to go with him to games and serve as the water boy for his high school baseball team. This was no small thing to sell to the school, and it was definitely an out-of-the-box idea, but he did it. After several meetings with both schools' administrators as well as my mother, the plan was presented to me. If I worked hard in school and did not get into any trouble, then as a reward I would get to be the water boy. This meant leaving school early for games as well as trips to McDonalds afterward.

To many young people, this would be amazing an amazing offer, but I was an outcast student that nobody wanted. Mr. Lee was willing to take a chance on me. I began going to the baseball games and hanging out with the cool high school kids. This was like heaven on earth; for the first time I started to see how so-called normal people lived.

This deal was a lot of work for Mr. Lee as he had to drive me home daily, which added an hour to his commute. During these rides, he was constantly encouraging me. He would work daily to convince me that I could do whatever I wanted with my life. He absolutely poured his soul into painting amazing and powerful strokes on the canvas of my life.

One day while at a baseball game, I was sitting in the dugout with the players. A man I had seen around a few times was there. He looked like a coach but was always just watching everything and not saying much. Before long, he started to ask me about my life. He asked about my school, my parents, and everything I had going on. He really took interest in me, and I remember feeling really cool. Then he started telling me that I should be playing football because I was big. I remember telling him that I couldn't play football because my school didn't have the sport available for middle school students. He shifted gears on me and came up with an idea that would change the trajectory of my life. He said he could arrange for me to play on his team, but he also asked whether I would work hard in school and on the field in order to play. I said sure but thought this deal was unlikely to happen.

I then came to find out that this man I had been speaking with was the

2   Names in this book have been changed to protect the individuals' identities.

varsity football coach for the local high school. He had more influence than I could have ever imagined. He got with Mr. Lee and the administration teams of the alternative school and the public school and set out a plan. At the time, it was spring. I had to maintain perfect behavior for the rest of the school year as well as stay out of trouble all summer. The reward for this would be that I would get bussed from the alternative school to the local public school every day for football practice.

Needless to say, this was a total game changer for me. Getting into trouble in school was no longer an issue for me. I had no more blow ups, no more suspensions, and no more tantrums. I had too much to lose. Playing football for the high school was a fantasy for me, and I was determined not to blow my shot.

- -ANSWER THESE QUESTIONS

What would have happened if Mr. Lee had not invested in me?

_____

_____

What would have happened if I had not taken the opportunity he was giving me?

_____

_____

Where would I be right now?

_____

_____

It scares me to think where I would be without this opportunity; I am sure things would not be good. I had to be willing to let these people invest in me, but I also needed those people to take that step.

How many people do you have in your life that are trying to help you but you are not letting them?

_____

_____

How many people could you be helping that you are not willing to reach out to?

_____

_____

My story is full of people investing in me. This is just one specific example. It would do all of us some good to take stock of the people in our lives and determine what role they play. The fact is that much like the canvas example from earlier in the chapter, people are always influencing us. The sooner we learn to utilize the great people in our lives, the sooner we can get on with our personal revolutions.

HOME INFLUENCES

One of the biggest challenges we have as people is that we often mislabel people who are simply challenging us as negative influences. At times we may feel like someone is all over our case when the fact of the matter is that this person is trying to help us. This is not a hard and fast rule, and each situation is unique. There are so-called haters out there for sure, but most of the time, the people who will help us the most are the ones that drive us nuts at times. We must learn to know ourselves enough to be honest with ourselves. We must challenge our self-image and attitude to ensure we are viewing people the right way.

Growing up in an abusive home and dealing with constant chaos trained me to deal with problems I had with people through violent acts. So when my mom introduced us to Chuck, the change was like a breath of fresh air for me. My mom did not date anyone for several years after my parents split up. Because of this, enough time went by where I was actually looking forward to her getting remarried. The classic line is be careful what you wish for; you just might get it.

When my Mom and Chuck were dating, everything was awesome. Chuck was always nice, and he would always do things with us. I still remember when my mom told us she and Chuck were getting married. We were so excited to have a real-life stepfather, and everything was nearly perfect before my mom and Chuck got married. Once they did, I became a handful for Chuck, and he was where I met my match.

In the dating phase, Chuck never had to deal with me and my horrible behavior like he did when I lived with him. I guess I was on my best behavior until my mom got married. Looking back on that time now, I honestly feel amazed that Chuck even took all of us on with such an amazing attitude. But he married my Mom, who had three kids—ages six, eight and twelve. At the time when Chuck and my mom got married, I was in a detention school and often in trouble with the law. Chuck is a modern-day hero, and I am still thankful that he stepped in, but it was not easy for either of us. He believed in me enough to invest all of himself into me. The things this man put up with still blow my mind today.

Chuck had a way of dealing with my violent behavior that was a far cry from what I was used to. One day I was talking to my Mom, and for whatever reason, I started yelling at her. Chuck calmly told me not to talk to my mother that way. I flipped out and started yelling at him and used a bunch of nasty language. He then calmly said to me that I couldn't talk to people like that. His calm demeanor just sent me off the deep end; I totally lost it! I swore at him and even used the classic line: "You're not my dad."

By that point, I was out of my mind with rage, and what Chuck did next enraged me even further; he started laughing at me. He did not mock. He just chuckled. There I was, blowing my lid, and he was laughing at me. Then he told me that I had a week of being grounded. He told me to stop and that if I kept going, there would be more punishment. I continued to scream. With a smile, he then upped my punishment to two weeks and said that if I wanted to keep going then so would he. I continued as my rage took over, and this went on until I had a month of being grounded.

The thing about being grounded by Chuck was that I had to do hard time. He was always home, so I always had to be home. That was a big problem for me when I was grounded. I couldn't have any friends over and couldn't go to my grandma's house or anywhere else for anything. But what Chuck did next would make me more frustrated than anything else.

When Chuck laid down the consequences, those were the consequences, and there was no getting out of them and no negotiation. I went to him begging for him to spank me instead; he would just say no. He said that I knew what I was doing and knew the punishment and did it anyway. A couple of weeks would go by, and again I would be begging. He just repeated himself and told me that I had to do my time. He did not say these things in a mocking or sarcastic manner at all; his tone just said this is how it is. Eventually he got tired of me begging, and in most cases, this is where the parents cave in. But not Chuck. When he got tired of my begging was when he said that every day I asked to have my time reduced, more time was added on to my punishment. If I begged, instead of letting me off, Chuck actually made my grounding last longer.

Anyone who has kids knows it is a lot of work to keep someone grounded. It takes a great amount of effort to keep up with the sentence you handed out. It would have been much easier for Chuck to just let me off. But to him it was important that I learn that my actions have consequences that cannot be negotiated out of. During the time I was grounded, Chuck would still come in each night and talk to me before bed. He would still joke around with me and was still nice, but the time was the time, and that was it.

There were several situations much like this one, and I still remember the last time I was grounded. Chuck had a frog pond behind the house, and he found out I had killed a bunch of the frogs. I killed them in several mean and nasty ways—ways that I am ashamed of to this day. Take all of the stories you hear about kids who grew up in the country and what they did to animals and double that. For what I did, I got a month of hard time. I tried to work on Chuck to get my punishment reduced, but his answer was always the same. If I complained, then I got more time.

For some silly reason, after my time was up I decided to do the same thing all over again. The next time I was grounded, there were several add-ons. Every day after school, I had to be in my room for two hours is one example. That time, I did not beg. I went to Chuck at the beginning and told him I was sorry that I killed a bunch of his frogs. I admitted that it was wrong and that I deserved the punishment. I no longer asked to have the sentence reduced; I just did my time. I truly felt bad for what I had done and felt true remorse for my actions.

Two weeks of my grounding went by, and Chuck blew my mind. He came out to the kitchen table and sat me down. Having explained to me why it was wrong the first time I did it, he didn't do that this time. He sat across from me and said that he thought I may have learned my lesson, and then he made an offer that if I gave him my word right then and there to never do anything like what I had done, then I was free. But if I did do it again, then I would get two months' time. I thought hard on that deal for just a moment, and then I promised I would never kill frogs again. Chuck reached out and shook my hand.

At the time I felt this was somewhat out of character for him. He had never let me off early before. But because I understood there was no way out and honestly felt bad that I let him down, I made a promise to myself as well as him that I would change. It was not the same surface type of promise that I had made before but one I knew in my heart I would not break.

A year later, I was mowing the lawn and accidentally hit a toad. I just about started crying because I felt like I had gone back on our deal.

Chuck knew what it would take to break me of my terrible behavior. It was not rage or anger that I needed but clear expectations and real and clear consequences. This lesson has helped me in more ways than I could ever imagine.

To say that Chuck changed my life for the better is an understatement. The fact is if he had not taken the hard road with me, then I would be in prison today. I had so many deep-rooted issues that nobody else had been able to break, but he had a great mix of love and respect to go along with a stubborn streak that was longer than my own.

There were times when I downright hated Chuck for the rules he enforced and punishment he delivered. I remember thinking that he hated me and that he came into my world and jacked it all up. He gave me all these stupid rules and punishments. I asked myself, "who in the world did he think he was?"

Once I started to learn that Chuck truly loved me, I understood that he loved me enough to be the bad guy. After a couple rocky years, I began to embrace his advice and seek it out all the time. He never held my past issues over my head. He always told me that I changed and that he didn't change me. He told me that I learned to make better choices.

Chuck is now not only my stepdad and the grandfather of my kids, he is one of my truest friends. The work he put into me in those dark times saved my life. When my wife and I had our first child and found out it was a boy, there was no doubt that I wanted to name him after Chuck. Charlie and his younger brothers will never know the hell my life was growing up because of the acts of this quiet hero. He was a force that changed the trajectory of my life forever.

-----------------------------------ANSWER THESE QUESTIONS

At times, the people in our lives who are the most difficult and most nagging are often the ones that we will be so happy we had in our lives later on down the road. Without them pushing and pushing on us, we would not be able to grow like we need to. It is essential that you take stock of your current situation. Think about the person that is always on your case.

Who is riding you?

_____

_____

Why are they riding you?

_____

_____

Do you think it is fun pushing and teaching and prodding a person to change?

_____

_____

Why else would they do it unless it was out of pure care for you?

_____

_____

- -

Parents, teachers, and coworkers are in our lives, and in many ways this is out of our control. We have a link to our parents for life and a link to our teachers due to school, and unless we want to change jobs, we can be somewhat stuck with our coworkers. If we elect to leave a job just to get away from people, unfortunately, we will most likely find similar people at our new job.

The people in our lives that we have minimal control over are always going to be there, but they influence us as much as we allow them to. Parents can make our lives seemingly smooth or rocky based on how they treat us, but the challenge for us as we grow up is to understand we have much more control than we think. Maybe you have a person in your life like my father was, like Chuck was, or like someone in the middle, but in both of these relationships, how I choose to view them impacted the influence they had on my life. The same is true for you. If someone is broken and you know it, that person cannot hurt you as much. If someone is trying to help you and you fail to utilize that help, you will most likely regret it as you get older. This thought process is great to utilize when we are young, but it is also mandatory as we grow older and join the workforce. You simply can't run from all bad influences, but you can manage them appropriately.

CHAPTER SEVEN
The People in Our Lives by Our Choice

Friends are people who are in our lives because we choose to be around them. These choices at the time may seem small, but they can tangle or untangle our lives depending on who we choose to be around. Aristotle has defined three distinct types of friends we have in our lives—utility, pleasure, and good.

Utility friends are friends we have for a season of our life because of proximity. They may be people we are in class with, work with, or play sports with. Once we graduate or the season is over, our friendship naturally dissolves due to the fact that our common interest is gone. This is not always the case; often we meet people in these circumstances and are lifelong friends, but more often than not these friends are in and out of our lives.

Pleasure friends are similar to casual friends, but in this case we have increasingly more of a choice to spend time with them. They are friends you have because you are into certain things at the same time. Some of the friends you had growing up you may have ridden bikes with or gone swimming with. As you get older, you have friends you party with. Once we grow out of bikes, no longer like swimming in the lake, or stop partying, these friendships often fade due to the fact that we outgrew the common interest. Just because you rode bikes with someone when you were ten years old doesn't mean you will vacation together with your families when you're older. Sometimes you will, but more times than not, you won't.

Good friends are the type of friendships you see poems or memes about. While this friendship is a great ideal, it is also the most rare. These types of friendships run deep. They bring joy to our lives that nothing can match.

In this type of relationship, there is a true, genuine care for the other person. You care for them as much as or more than yourself. Unlike the utility friends and pleasure friends, these friends don't require that common interest to keep that bond. A good friend is one that you can sit with and talk to for hours while the time just slips away. This is a friend that you are truly happy for when they are doing well and truly sad for when they struggle. Time is not a factor with this type of friend. You could go six months without seeing them, and when you get together, it is as if you hang out every day.

These friendships are so rare that many times we only have a few of them in our lives. I recently went to meet one of my friends from this category for breakfast. We had not spoken in five months. We met for breakfast at nine in the morning, and when we left the restaurant, it was two in the afternoon. It felt like we were there for five minutes. We both left feeling encouraged, energized, and entertained. These friends put a new light in our lives when they are around.

IT IS UP TO YOU

The thing people often say about people who are going down a bad path is that they are running with a bad crowd. This term is referring to the fact that the person making the statement understands the influence that the people around us have. The problem arises when we fail to notice this influence and act accordingly. If we are running with a bad crowd, we must realize the problem and take total ownership of it.

Friends in all three of these categories are influencing us, and in many cases. they can help us with our personal revolution. But there will also be many friends that simply will not help us; in fact, they will pull us backward on our journey. We must evaluate these relationships consistently to ensure we are moving in the right direction.

While there are very few friendships that last a lifetime, there are many more that come and go. It is essential for us to look at the fading or abrupt ending of a friendship in the proper light.

"A prudent man, remembering that life is short, examines his friendships critically now and then. A few he retains, but the majority he tries to forget." –H.L. Mencken[3]

----

3   Earl Nightingale and Robert C. Worstell, *How to Change Your Life in 30 Seconds – Compleat* (Midwest Journal Press, 2017), 148.

The view that H.L. Mencken highlights in the quote above is huge as it relates to our personal revolution. We must understand that it is not always a bad thing when the well of friendship runs dry with someone. In many cases, the end of a friendship is just what we need in our lives. If you are working on your life and consistently growing, you will outgrow people and some will outgrow you. This does not make you better than them or them better than you; this is just part of growing in life. We often look at the end of a friendship as a divorce or a termination from a job we once loved. But it is something that, as we grow older, is essential for our growth.

As I went through the many seasons of my life, I had many people who I spent large amounts of time with and who, as time went on and my life changed, no longer fit in my life. Sometimes the end of a friendship is completely unintentional, and other times there must be a deliberate break.

Sometimes we have people in our lives and one day it hits us that they are not people we want to be around anymore. Sometimes we have to almost break up with them.

I had a friend growing up that I would spend time with, and we had fun together. As young boys, we would play on his father's farm and go off into the woods and knock over trees. As we grew older, the things we did together changed. We went from playing as kids together to playing sports together as teens.

Once we got into high school, this friend began to adopt a party-filled lifestyle. When he called me, it was often clear that he had been drinking. During this season of my life, this was not behavior that I participated in. I stayed close to him because I felt that I wanted to help him with his challenges. He was regularly trying to get me to party with him, but at that time, I knew those parties were trouble.

A few years after college, I began to drink on occasion and started to hang out with this friend again. We would go out and have a good time, and on many occasions, it felt like old times; however, I began to notice that this friend did not seem to ever slow down when he was partying. He eventually got himself into some legal trouble as a result of his lifestyle. I went to visit him in prison and shared with him how I had outgrown that lifestyle. While I had partied with him, it had been a phase I had gone through and had since moved on from. While he was in prison, he said he was ready to move on as well.

Once this friend got out, I set him up with a job with someone I knew. I spent time with him and even arranged for a place for him to live after he got out of prison. He was an old friend who I cared for deeply, and I felt an obligation to help him through his challenges. But he was not done with his old lifestyle. He began to drink heavily again and soon burned all the bridges I had helped build for him. He was not only being reckless with his life but also taking advantage of my generosity; I had put my neck on the line for him.

I talked to him about it one day when I once again visited him while he served another jail term, it became clear to me that this friend was not someone I wanted to spend any more time with. I could tell by the way he spoke that he did not take responsibility in any way for his situation. He was going to get out and do the same thing again. I had helped him all I could and had to decide to move on. It was costing me too much energy to be his friend.

I felt terrible but finally came to the conclusion that I had to cut my old friend loose. I didn't call him and blast him about his life choices; he knew how I felt already. I also wanted to be fair to him, and blowing him off didn't seem fair. I simply told him that I didn't think it was a good idea for he and I to spend time together anymore. I wished him nothing but the best and hoped that he would have an amazing future.

That situation was very difficult to be in, but at times we must draw that line in the sand and deal with the people that are hurting us, even if the issue is just that they are always bumming us out. Once you have gotten to the point where you can honestly say to yourself that you have been a good friend to this person and have done everything you can to help this person and the situation has now shifted to your friend pulling you down rather than you lifting your friend up, you have to deal with it.

I remained civil, and off and on, I have sent him an email, but the constant communication went away. He is doing well now, and we are not enemies in any way; we just grew apart.

This is not to say that when a friend is going through a challenge we just cut them off. This would not be being a good friend on our part. It is up to each of us to make our own assessments of the people in our lives. Some we will keep, and some we will lose, and that is okay.

-------------------------------------ANSWER THESE QUESTIONS

Can you think of a few people in your life that it may be time to move on from?

_____

_____

Do you need to have some difficult discussions with a few people?

_____

_____

Who are these people? When can you have these discussions?

_____

_____

- -

THERE IS SOMETHING BETTER

One of the biggest challenges we have with cutting people loose is falling into the trap of thinking that we need to have someone to hang out with, or we say to ourselves that we would rather put up with someone than be by ourselves.

This is a lie; it is simply not true. There are people out there who can be great friends to you. They can build you up and encourage you and be a positive light. We cannot find them if we are stuck in the mud with someone we are tolerating just so we don't have to pass the time alone.

Do you have time to spend with someone that is always dragging you down? Maybe you do, but I don't, and if you are honest with yourself, you don't either. Money lost can be restored, and things lost can be replaced, but time is a commodity that cannot be replaced. Think on that when you are choosing to spend time with someone. In the next chapter, we will dig into ways we can strategically put people in our lives to help us grow.

CHAPTER EIGHT
Role Models

We have defined the types of people we have in our lives as well as the influence they all have. It has been made clear that at times we may need to move on from people who are dragging us backward. Once we identify the negative influences and begin removing them, we must work to be strategic and intentional about the people we have in our lives.

Remember the example about the canvas? Now we will start to dig into ways you can pick who paints on your canvas.

I recently read a quote from Jim Rohn in John C. Maxwell's *15 Invaluable Laws of Growth* that says "you are the average of the five people you spend the most time with.[4]"

There are many quotes that reflect a similar truth; we are who we spend our time with. But who should we spend our time with? This question is something you should spend some good time thinking through. This question and your answer can have a massive impact on your personal revolution or the lack thereof.

When thinking about who we can seek out as a positive influence, the first thing many of us think is *who has what I want?* While this is an understandable first question, a more fitting one would be *who lives the way I want to live?* It is not so much what people have as it is the way they live that should draw us to them. The world is full of people who have big homes and nice cars but who may not be a good influence. Of course, many people with big homes and nice cars could be good influences, but the fact that they

---

4   John C. Maxwell, *15 Invaluable Laws of Growth* (Hachette Book Group, 2012).

have these things does not automatically make them a person whom you want to learn from. The opposite is true as well. We can often learn a great deal from our relationships with people who have little in the possessions department. In the important areas of life, how are your influences doing? Do they live with integrity? Do they have a family life that we admire? Do they treat others with respect? People come in all shapes and sizes, and the ones we are around are influencing us. We must learn to look at traits we respect and follow those traits.

In my life, I have found many people that live how I want to live, and I spend as much time as I can listening to them when they give me advice.

MENTORING RELATIONSHIPS

Several different men have stood in the gap that the absence of my father created. What is interesting is that as I have grown older, the list of men who have had massive influence on me has grown as well.

As a youth, that gap was filled by my stepdad and grandpa, and as I grew older, I grew close to a couple of uncles. As an adult, I am still close to these people, but other figures have emerged.

One example of these father figures is one uncle I have grown increasingly close to over the past years as I have gotten married and had kids. He is a friendly man, but as I was growing up, I was certainly intimidated by him. My fear was no fault of his; he is just a no-nonsense kind of person, and for whatever reason, I never really spent much time talking to him on a personal level.

As got older and progressed in life, I began to notice his life more. I noticed the relationship he had with his wife and with his kids, and I began to take notice that he was a guy who had his life together. He was a person who knew what he wanted, had a plan, and was working on that plan.

Not long after I married, I found myself in a situation where I was in some serious need of financial advice. I went to my uncle and humbly asked for only one thing, which was his opinion on how I could fix the situation. My wife and I took his advice and ran with it. We read the books he suggested, and we adopted the mindset he suggested. Our financial situation is as different as night and day from what it was on the day that I called my uncle out of desperation. He did not give money; that was not what I asked for or needed. He gave me something better. He gave me knowledge.

Even before I got married, my uncle had a very long talk with me about managing the in-law relationship. While my in-laws are the best in-laws in the history of the world, I am still thankful for the knowledge he gave me. We often see our world from our own perspective, and by using his knowledge, I was able to take a lot of strain out of my future by understanding other people's perspectives.

At times, my uncle has a blunt way of putting things, and his frankness may not feel good to hear at the time. In one specific situation, he gave me some very tough and challenging feedback about the direction I was going in life. At the time, his words had hurt me deeply, but then I began to think. A question came to me that helped shape how I took this painful advice: *what does he have to gain by telling me this?*

If someone tells you something that hurts, ask what they have to gain by telling you such a thing. I pondered this question and found that in my situation, my uncle had nothing to gain by telling me what he had said. After further thought, I realized he most likely did not want to tell me what he did. Then it all hit me. He told me the truth because he cared. He told me the truth because he had the courage to. It would have been far easier for him not to address the situation. My frustration over what he told me went away, and it was replaced with thankfulness for the advice. After I went through this thought process, I concluded that my uncle's advice was very accurate and that I should heed it. This shift in thinking toward the advice I receive has been key in my personal revolution.

People can give you all the advice in the world, but if you fail to take it, you are still responsible for your situation. We can tell a child over and over that the stove is hot, but it often takes the sting of the heat before the child understands. Listening to these key people in our lives may not always be easy, but it will help us avoid unnecessary pain.

Don't be the kid who has to touch the heat; listen to the people who love you and care about you. But if you are like me, you may have to get burned a few times before you start to listen. That is okay, too. Pain is a great teacher, but it is not the only way to learn.

BE COACHABLE

Sports are full of great metaphors for life. One that is very relevant to this is the player-coach relationship. In many ways, the people in our lives that we look to are like coaches. The key idea is that a coach wants what is best for the player and the team, and the player wants what is best for the coach and the team.

The player and the coach only win if each person is successful in the role they have. A coach may get on a players case about making a mistake, but the player knows the only way he can help the team win is to listen to his coach. Just like many of the people in our lives, sometimes the player is frustrated with the coach and struggles. It is often only after a few head-to-head battles with each other that they finally learn to understand the other's intentions. Once each person understands the other's intent is in each other's best interest, they are able to help each other. Neither can win without the other.

One of the largest roadblocks we will ever face when dealing with people who try to help us in our journey is our own ego. I know a great amount of content has been written about building our self-image and improving how we see ourselves, but there is also a flip side to this coin.

It is a serious problem if, when somebody speaks wisdom to us about our lives, we think to ourselves *who are you to tell me what I need to do with my life?* This thought will sabotage us for our entire lives. There are times when people tell us things we may not like and is not good advice, but there are also many times when we need to humble ourselves.

The best way to manage this internal struggle is, as mentioned before, to ask yourself the question *what does this person have to gain by telling me this?* Asking yourself this question will help unpack whether the advice given is advice that is not for you or whether your ego is robbing you of the wisdom someone is trying to share with you.

ROLE MODELS PUSH US

If the people that we feel are role models in our lives never push us or challenge us, then they are more friends than role models. A person can be both, of course, but unless these people pull us out of our comfort zones from time to time, they are more like buddies that we hang out with than coaches who make us better.

How many times have we seen coaches who lose control of their team and then get fired on the first day of the off season? This happens every year. Think about any bosses you have had that have been let go. They may not have not stepped up or put their foot down or driven results, and as a result, the organization's performance has slipped, so their boss has to deal with them.

That is not to say that a role model is someone who only gives you negative feedback; the point is that if you are not getting pushed, the person is not an effective role model. That is not to say this person is a bad person or not a good friend and has no value in your life. It simply means that your friend is not the ideal role model to help you get better.

DIFFERENT ROLE MODELS FOR DIFFERENT THINGS.

Some of the people we can learn from may help us greatly in one area and not so much in another. This does not mean we disregard someone's help; it just means that we must pick the areas we want to model and the areas we want to leave alone.

I remember one season of my life when I was struggling at work. I was doing my job in a satisfactory manner but was struggling with my relationship with my boss. I was in a constant state of trying to gain approval. Many of the struggles I was dealing with were more related to personal issues. They had very little to do with the workplace. I had a peer who was a huge help to me. He taught me how to believe in myself at work and how to get my personal life back on track. As a result, he was instrumental in a huge shift in my thinking, and I have never had those issues at work since. I just think back to his advice, and I am almost instantly free again from those thoughts.

This man had been divorced three times and was buried in debt and continued to make poor financial decisions. I watched him and kept thinking *what are you doing, man?*

The point is, he was able to give me great advice in a specific area of my life, but in other ways I had to disregard his advice. Rarely do we meet someone who has it all together in every aspect of their life. If I had focused on his shortcomings and his past failures, I would have disregarded his life-changing advice.

During this same season of my life, I was dealing with some financial concerns that were adding a whole bunch of stress to my life. I had another person who helped me deal with this issue. He taught me how to think differently and how to attack debt and how to see a way out. My family's financial outlook is 180-degrees different now than it was in that season of my life. The man who helped me financially, however, is not one to give personal advice.

In my examples, one person was very helpful in one area of life, while another was very helpful in another area. Role models are rarely a one-stop shop of help to us. Similarly, a football coach has two running backs; one is big and strong and can pound the football for that one yard needed for a first down, while the other running back is small and quick and can find space to take the ball all the way for the score. Each one is great at what they do, but if you reverse their roles, they are not nearly as effective. The big, strong one does not have the skills to break for the long run, and the small, quick one would struggle to get that final yard. Each is an expert in their area.

Role models in our lives are very similar. Just as an example, we may have people in our lives to help us immensely with our faith, but we may want to ignore their financial advice. There may be others who are great with marriage advice but not so good with job-related advice. That is not to say that people who manage their marriage well cannot be good workers; it is more to say that we must determine what advice to take from who. In many ways, this would be similar to going to a buffet for dinner. You may go and select several items that you like and leave others. You don't have to eat everything on the buffet. You get what you like and leave the rest. Life-changing advice is much more valuable than a trip to the buffet, but the idea is that you take what works for you and leave the rest. This does not mean the rest of the food is garbage; it just means you prefer something else. Each diner at the buffet will select different things that work for them.

The key to this whole thought process working for you is to remember the canvas example from before. If you know what you want your canvas to look like, you can utilize different painters with different skills. If you have no clue what you want your canvas to look like, then you are still open to people destroying it.

Even when you have great people in your life, you still own your canvas. Your personal revolution requires that you own it. You cannot just latch on to someone else and listen to every word they say and follow them step by step. You must decide what you want your canvas to look like. What do you want for your life? Figure that out, and then find people who can help you get there.

- -ANSWER THESE QUESTIONS

Do you know what you want your canvas to look like?

_____

_____

What is your ultimate vision for your life?

_____

_____

Who do you know who could be great to paint on this canvas?

_____

_____

- -

FIND YOUR ROLE MODELS NOW

The necessity of finding role models at a young age makes developing and maintaining relationships while you are still in school even more important. As I often tell high school and college students, dream now, find NOW what you want to do with your life, and find the role models now. The reason is that while you are in school, you have people in your life who have chosen a field where helping people live their dreams is their job. Not every teacher is this way, but you are much more likely to encounter these types of people in school than when you get out into the workforce. You are surrounded by people who have spent and often borrowed tens of thousands of dollars to be certified to teach and train people. If they went through all that expense and work, they likely have a passion for helping others. Helping you and watching you grow is their payoff. Watching you succeed validates their passion and is a priceless reward for them.

When people are out of school and in the workplace, it is much more difficult to find people to sow into their dream field. That is not to say those people are not there; they are just much more difficult to find. Once people go into the workforce, they are focused on the job, the tasks involved, and the profitability of not only their company but themselves. This is not a negative shot at anyone; it is just a fact. A boss's job is to teach and train you to perform a duty for your company to earn money, not necessarily to help you live your dreams, which may not have anything to do with the job you have at the time.

At this point, people often have their family and children they are sowing into. While some seek to sow into the lives of others, in most cases people are at work to work, and they do their work to help others at home. In relation to educators, their job is to help people—not to produce more widgets at a low price to drive profit for their company.

There can be great role models in the workplace, though, and at times it may seem like some educators are not good role models. Regardless of where we are in our lives, we are responsible to find our role models. The likelihood of finding a good one in an education setting is simple math equation; your percentages of success are higher.

To summarize this thought process, a good role model has a desire to help people and takes great joy in doing so, and you can give to them as much as you get from them. The sooner you start to identify what you want to do and who can help you, the more likely you are to find your role models.

CHAPTER NINE
Give and Take

Over the two previous chapters, you have learned about the amazing value of the role-model relationship. One thing to keep in mind as you learn to look at the people around you is that all healthy relationships involve a give and take. You need to challenge yourself to not just be a taker. A taker is a person that is always looking at a relationship to find what is in it for themselves. They often have no desire to make it a two-way relationship.

There are people who can make you better and whom you can learn from, but why would someone want to invest so much into another person? As you learn to build relationships with people who can help you, you will learn that some people want to do it while others do not. Finding someone who finds a great amount of joy helping others is a key aspect of finding a good role model.

A good role model that pushes you and directs you can take as much away from the relationship as you can. One great example of this is as I go to different parts of the country and speak to students, I often have them come up to me after the program and share with me how much my story has helped and inspired them. Hearing these stories gives me a great sense of value to the work I have put in to becoming a speaker. It helps me see that I am making a difference and that I must keep going. Through sharing my personal challenges and victories with people and helping them with their challenges, I find myself more strengthened in my own battles. We all have challenges and issues. Nobody is perfect, and a great lift is provided to the role models as they see how their past pains and challenges can help someone else. In many ways, I gain as much as I give when speaking to students. In some ways it is like my therapy.

You may also have a ton to bring to the relationship that you may not realize. While a mentor may be very good at marriage advice but not so good at financial advice, you may struggle with marriage issues but be a wiz with your money. So in many cases, the advice can go back and forth. These are the best situations because you and your role model are truly making each other better.

As I have grown older and had my own family, I have often reached out to teachers from my past and touched base with them. When I reach out to them or just run into them by accident, I am amazed at the praise they heap upon me about the challenges I have overcome. In many cases, I have forgotten how messed up I was, but they remember me when I was riddled with personal problems. While doing an interview with one of my old teachers for a teacher revolution program I have, I asked her what it meant to her now to see what my life is like and know she as there for me before things turned around.

That was when the rubber hit the road, so to speak. Her eyes lit up, and her smile spread from ear to ear. She said, to sum it up, that it brought her an overwhelming joy. Seeing that all the hours and emotional energy she put into me paid off provided her with a joy that cannot be bought or sold; it can only be earned.

It can be difficult to invest in someone. You will have role models to whom, at times, you are somewhat taxing. But when they see that work and energy pay off, you will give them the greatest gift you can. By listening to your role models and following the right steps, you help validate their work. You give them the opportunity to look in the mirror and say to themselves that they really made a difference or that this person is better off for having known them. This is not an arrogant or conceited thing to say to oneself; it is something we all hope to be able to honestly say to ourselves. To give that to one of our role models is an amazing gift.

GIVE BACK

As a person who has had multiple personal revolutions at varying stages of my life because of the work of others, I feel an obligation to do the same for others. One way I choose to do this is by speaking to students and meeting with them often after the presentations. I do this because it provides me with a great amount of joy and fulfillment. I also do it because I can and should.

If you have overcome a great difficulty in your life, just know there are many people all around you that are still fighting the same battle you have won before. I have many cousins in my family that have challenges similar to mine. Whenever I get a chance, I drop them a line of encouragement or ask them how things are going for them. This often leads to a great conversation in which they learn from my mistakes. I get a feeling of joy as I watch them take this advice. Many of them are now getting married and often tell me that my family is an inspiration to them. As mind blowing as it is to me, they look from a distance at my life, and in many ways it is a goal for them. This is a reminder that we are always being watched by someone and that helping them is not only fun and rewarding but also our duty.

I am not saying that you should give away money or spend all your extra time trying to chase down people who you can preach to about their problems. Giving back is more about making yourself available. Be available and let people know you are available, and the ones who want to learn from you will come to you.

All aspects of life are made up of give and take, from parenting and marriage to the workplace. Life is a constant give and take from paying money for items and services to maintaining relationships. At times, being a taker is what you need, but when you can be a giver, you need to embrace this role and do it as much as possible.

There is a lifetime of opportunities to help others, and you don't have to train to be a professional speaker to help either. You can be one of the people in your school or workplace who find joy in helping others.

Several years back, I went to work at a facility and became a peer to a fellow manager. She was struggling at work and had a great amount of pressure on her to improve her performance. She was being written up by our boss and was working in a constant state of fear for her job. She was a single mother, and this added a great amount of pressure. I took a special interest in this peer and spent time with her too talk about the job. I went over the ins and outs of the things I do differently from her. It was clear that she had a teachable attitude and wanted to grow. I also spent a great deal of time helping her learn how to manage the relationship with our boss. She was scared of him and had thought that he was gunning for her, which is a very common mindset of people who are getting written up. As I began to spend time with her, I shared with her that the boss was simply doing his job. He was honestly on her side, but his job required him to push her and prod her and make her better.

After working with her for a couple of months, she began to grow and develop. She grew in her job performance, and she also began to foster that relationship with this boss that she had at one point thought was gunning for her. After six months or so, I was promoted to another position within the company and was no longer going to be working with her. She pulled me aside on my last day and said that she just wanted to thank me for all of my help. She said she would not be where she was without my help. That statement meant more to me than the promotion I had just received. She has since been promoted several times within the same company. Her and the boss no longer work together, but they still have a role-model relationship and are very close.

I am not going to take all the credit for turning this person around; she did it. I will say that watching her turn the corner and become a great leader provides me with a great sense of accomplishment, especially as I think of where she was when we first met. It also inspires me to continue to be available to people. You may be able to help reveal the answer to a life problem for someone else, and you could change that person's life. Your job is to be available.

Helping others live their dreams is a great undertaking, but in some cases, you are just helping people survive the storm. Either one is a great task that at times can be taxing but is more than worth it. After it is all said and done, in many cases, the role model gains more than they gave. This is why people who become very wealthy often give large sums of money away; they feel compelled to see their hard work go to help others. Sometimes help is money, but often it is just a listening ear and some well-placed advice that make the biggest difference.

HOW TO BE A ROLE MODEL

Newsflash, you already are a role model because people are always watching. Your friends, family, kids, and coworkers are all watching. Don't live in fear of this; take it as inspiration to show them how life is done. The biggest thing is to *show* them and not always to *tell* them.

In answer to the question of how to be a role model, the first step is to make yourself available. This is more a of a mindset than a task you perform. Being aware of the people around you and being mindful of what they have going on is how you make yourself available. Whether in school or work, you are no doubt surrounded by people who are having a hard time in an area of life that you have figured out. Ask people how they are doing; ask them if they are okay today. Simple questions begin the process. Once people begin to open up to you, keep asking them questions.

IT'S NOT ABOUT YOU

One theory in management that also works well with personal concerns is the 5 Whys exercise. It was developed by Toyota to identify operational issues within their company. It is a very simple idea. Once someone identifies a problem, you ask why. By the 5th time you ask why, you will have identified the root cause of the issue. The great thing about the 5 Whys is you get to the root cause quickly. An even better aspect of it is the person who is bringing you the problem is also bringing the solution to the problem. By asking the other person questions, you help that person slow down, think on the issue, and do most of the talking. A person can listen to you for an hour, but if they listen to the answer come out of their own mouth in five minutes, it can rock their world more than all the talking you could do in a month.[5]

Using this exercise when helping others not only helps people more efficiently and quickly but also prevents you from turning into a soapbox preacher—the person who is always telling others what to do and how to do it. Nobody likes that person, and certainly nobody goes to that person for advice on personal matters. People will, however, go to the person who listens actively and asks good questions that help them find answers. You must remember that when a person is coming to you with their problem they are not coming to you to hear you talk; they are coming to you to solve their problem. This is a time when you must remind yourself that not everything is not about you; in this case, it is about the other person. Knowing that and playing to that when you go in makes the whole encounter and relationship go the way it should.

When it is your turn to share your life with others, you must remember your failures in the correct sense as learnings. If you look at your past mistakes as a millstone around your neck, you will never be able to help someone else with similar issues; however, if you look at these events as great learning seasons of your life, you can parlay that into a great lesson for a person who needs advice. This is how helping other people can almost be therapy for you.

---

5   Jeffrey K. Liker, *The Toyota Way* (McGraw Hill, 2004), 253.

Life is made up of a constant give and take. It is important for all of us to develop a healthy balance between the two, much like in the way you would play tennis with someone. You hit the ball to the other person, and your partner hits it back to you. The ball goes back and forth, and each person gets a turn to hit the ball as well as react to the ball being hit toward them. No person who always takes can be truly happy because they are broken. No person who always gives can be truly happy as they are also broken. If a person is always taking, then they are not using the advice they are being given. The person who always gives will become depleted and wear down over time from giving constantly without replenishing. A healthy balance is key. A healthy balance at one season of your life might be more take and less give. You will also have seasons where you are giving more than you are taking. There is no exact formula to determine this, but theoretically, in our younger years, we will be doing more taking, and as we grow older, we will be giving more.

- -ANSWER THESE QUESTIONS

There is a whole world of people out there. Some of them can help you live your dreams, while others you may help to live theirs. How we relate to others, good or bad, has a massive influence on our lives. If we want to live the lives we dream about, we must look for all the amazing people out there just waiting to help us along the way. While we take on our journey, we have a duty to give back to others. A life well lived is full of great, meaningful relationships. These relationships take work and effort, but it is in this space where life is enjoyed the most.

Right now, who do you have in your life that you can make yourself available to?

_____

_____

What failures do you have in your past that could help someone else?

_____

_____

- -

CHAPTER TEN
What Are You Thinking?

A s I talk to groups all over the place, people consistently ask me how I changed. I often tell them about different aspects of the change, but as I have grown older, the time when I changed has become increasingly clear to me.

My personal revolution type change happened when I learned to think of a life beyond my challenges. I learned to think of a life beyond the alternative school. I learned to think of a life beyond getting the bad grades, being teased at school, and hurting emotionally all the time. I learned to think of a life beyond being over 400 pounds and being broke.

I may have used the word *think* too many times in that paragraph, but I did so on purpose. Thinking is something that we often underrate. We fail to think about what we are thinking.

While we touched on this in other chapters, it would do all of us some good to analyze the thoughts in our head and realize that they will produce results. I have to chuckle when I see memes online that say things like *whether you think you can or think you can't, you're right.* We often view these memes and move on, but a personal revolution is when you say *ah-ha* and actually realize that no statement could be truer. It may be cliché and corny, but it is a fact. Looking at the power of our thoughts properly can be the single key we need to unlock all the doors of our dream life.

Our thoughts lead us to things. They lead us to the way we see ourselves as well as our own world. They lead us to how we see others and how we see our future. The one theme that is in every chapter of this book is how we think and view things in our lives. Thinking about thinking is mandatory to a personal revolution.

This idea is not one that I came up with; it is a principal that is as old as time. It was examined deeply by Earl Nightingale in his essay "The Strangest Secret." Earl grew up during the Great Depression and was always an avid reader. He joined the military to see the world and go on his quest, which was to figure out the reason one person can be happy while the other is miserable or how one person can grow up on the same block as another and be successful while the other is a failure as an adult.

Earl took to studying all the great books. He went on to study all the great religions of the world to look for his answer. All of the great thinkers over the years had many things they disagreed on, but there was one thread that they all shared in common. It was one idea that they all agreed upon as being absolutely essential to a person living a good life. Finding this thread is easy, but it is right in front of us, so we often miss it. This is why Earl called it the strangest secret.

The secret is "we become what we think about.[6]"

The challenges you are facing are your challenges, but there are others out there who have had the same challenges and have overcome them. How did these people overcome their challenges? They thought about the challenges differently and began to act accordingly. The earlier section on self-image is all about thought. The earlier section on attitude is all about thought. The section on the role of others is all about thought. The remaining sections of the book are about thought.

OUR THOUGHTS SHAPE OUR LIVES

One of the greatest books about the power of our thinking is *As a Man Thinketh* by James Allen.

James unpacks several elements of our thought life, but for the sake of our goals, we will focus on the fact—not the theory but the fact—that our thoughts shape our lives.

"Let a man radically alter his thoughts, and he will be astonished at the rapid transformation it will have in the material conditions of his life.[7]"

A great way to identify the manifestation of our thoughts shaping our lives is following the journey of a thought. First our thoughts become our

---

6 Earl Nightingale and Robert C. Worstell, *How to Change Your Life in 30 Seconds – Compleat* (Midwest Journal Press, 2017), 6.
7 James Allen, *As a Man Thinketh* (Longmeadow Press, 2009), 8.

words, and then our words become our actions, and finally our actions shape our lives. That journey sounds so simple, but it is true just the same.

It is most beneficial for all of us to begin learning about the power of our thoughts early on. If we learn to think about our thinking, we will be able to more accurately shape our lives. It is not possible to dream appropriately without understanding the power of our thoughts.

I recently took a drive down the west coast, from Seattle to Los Angeles. As I checked the map app now and then, I found it interesting to see all of the different directions I could take. I had a route and stuck to it, but if I had so chosen, I could have gone on thousands of different roads. Each road would have taken me in a different direction to a different destination. Our thoughts are much like these roads. Life can throw all kinds of alternate routes in our path, and it is up to us to understand the rules of the road and stay on the right route. What we often fail to do with our thoughts is think about where they will take us. Like the roads on the map, some will get us where we want to go while others will not. The trick for us to get where we want to go is to think about our thinking.

Imagine your thoughts and follow them through to their conclusion to see whether your current thoughts are on the right path. For example, let's pretend you and some of your friends decide to rent a cottage on the lake. These friends are some of your best friends, but you have never shared a home with them for any period of time. One of your friends starts to get on your nerves; maybe she leaves the bathroom a mess each morning, or maybe she chews with her mouth open. She does something trivial, and the first day it strikes you, but as the week goes on it, annoys you more and more. Then naturally other things start to annoy you about this friend; she snores or texts while you are talking to her. By the end of the week, you can't even stand to look at this person. In several ways, just having this person on the vacation with you has ruined your vacation.

What would have happened if, on the first day that you noticed the bathroom was a mess, you either softly said something to your friend or, better yet, just decided to let it go? You are only living with her for a week, and how often are you actually in the bathroom during that time? We get to make that choice with our thoughts. Once we learn to identify that following some thoughts through to their conclusion results in disaster, we learn to put our focus elsewhere. This person is the same friend who is always there for you when you call all hours of the night and the one who encourages you when you are down. When dealing with ourselves and others, we get to choose our thoughts. Since our thoughts are like roads, we must learn to challenge them and ensure they are getting us to an ideal destination.

Much like the human body, the human mind must be fed consistently if it is to perform at the highest level. Rarely will our thoughts take us to the ideal destination without us taking strategic action to ensure our minds are fed properly. It would be like me taking the route down the west coast and not having a map. I could end up in all kinds of different spots if I had no clear direction or path. We must decide where we want our thoughts to go and fill our minds accordingly. Traps lie out there for all of us. There are things we can do that will diminish our ability to think positively and creatively.

Have you ever started watching a show on Netflix and the next thing you know you just watched four or five episodes? When you finally turn it off, don't you feel like your brain is a little mushy? Then when you go to bed, you lay in bed thinking about the characters in the show and wonder where the next episode will take them. This happens to all of us, and while watching shows can be a great way to unwind, this habit gone unchecked fills our minds with useless information. Rather than thinking about our goals, our dreams, or our friends, we end up wrapped up in a fictional world that produces no real results. In some ways, falling into a Netflix hole is almost like making a choice to sedate ourselves.

Binge-watching TV is just one of the many traps we can fall into. Others could be logging too many hours playing video games or surfing social media too much. What would happen if you spent a portion of that time listening to a good podcast or reading a good book? What if, instead of watching that extra two or three episodes, you went to bed early and got up early to work out? This would lead to you being more rested, and the endorphins in the morning would give you a great rush to launch into a productive day. One path can build a positive and powerful thought life, and one will do the opposite. It is up to each of us to make our own choices about what we fill our minds with, but the key for us is to know that what we sow into our minds, we will certainly reap.

HOPE OR FEAR?

As we look at the power of our thoughts and their impact on our future, let's first look into the main motivators we have as people to drive change in our lives. Any significant life change we make that truly changes things is done from the inside out. When thinking about why we want to set a goal or how our life will be if we reach that goal, we will be motivated by one of two factors—hope or fear.

Fear is a common way we as people drive ourselves. If you, as a student, don't do this or that, you will get detention, suspended, or become a bum. As an employee, doing this or that will get you fired as well as cause you to lose your house and become a bum. For some dealing with the ultimate darkness of depression, fear is not an effective form of motivation because some simply don't care. People don't care whether they get suspended, locked up, or fired. They don't care whether they become a bum. The darkness can overtake them, and fear simply does not work. Fear is a negative emotion, and while in some cases it does spur us to change, it is a negative experience.

If you are truly hopeless internally as I was before my personal revolution, you cannot be driven by fear because you feel as if you having nothing to lose. Hope, on the other hand, is the opposite of fear. Hope gives light to the dark room you are living in. Hope helps you believe you can be better today than you were yesterday.

Hope to the student looks like this: do this or do that, and you get to pick your own college and choose what you want to do with your life. Hope to the employee is if you do this or that and do it well, then you will get to determine your own future. You will be in control of your career; you will be able to buy your dream house and drive the car you want. Hope and fear are two massive motivators for people, and we are all inspired by them often without knowing it. It would do all of us some good to stop for a moment and think on this.

Being motivated by fear or hope is another choice we all get to make when we are shaping our lives. If you are the student that is motivated by fear to not become a bum, you are shaping a negative experience. You envision yourself living in a van down by the river to move yourself to take action. Hope is the opposite, where you think about your dream house and financial security. What journey will be the most fun? When we want to envision our motivation for doing the work required, do we want to think about living in a van or our dream house? Both fear and hope can motivate us as humans, but one is much more fun. Since our motivation is a choice, it makes sense to choose hope; it will fill us with joy while doing the work required, whereas fear will make the work miserable. It still may get done, but it won't be as much fun, and in many cases this can lead us to giving up on our goals.

While the internal battle in our thoughts between hope and fear is common to all people, some have cracked the code while others have not. I once heard the story of an old Eskimo who had two dogs in the arctic. In the village there was a competition each week to test the dogs' strength and endurance. The Eskimo took his two dogs to the event each week, and each week a different dog won. The interesting thing was that he always seemed to bet correctly on the competition. The dog he bet on won every week. Finally someone asked the Eskimo how he knew each week which dog to bet on and he simply said that he just bet on the dog he has been feeding all week. The idea is that hope and fear are like the two dogs. They both have a massive amount of power but only as much power as we feed them. If we are struggling with fear, it is most likely because we are feeding that dog the most. If we are living a life of hope for the future, it is safe to say that is where the food is going. By choosing where we put our focus and where we direct our thoughts, we are having a direct impact on which motivator we are allowing to run our lives.

While we get to choose which dog to feed with our focus, we have many others ways we make that choice as well. For example, if we watch the news constantly and read about all the problems in the world to keep up to speed on every new health crisis and imagine its impact on us, we are feeding the dog of fear. We are conditioning our thoughts to think about massive problems that we have little or no control over. The other option is to spend our time reading or listening to good podcasts about things we enjoy. To feed our hope, we should learn new things and meet new people that we can allow into our lives to help us focus more on positive things. This new learning and focus gives the hope dog all kinds of energy.

- -ANSWER THIS QUESTION

Are you motivated by fear or hope?

_____

_____

- -

CHAPTER ELEVEN
The Value of Goals

"A man without a goal is like a ship without a rudder."
–Earl Nightingale[8]

No company that performs at a high level does so without a goal. No person that is happy and successful does so entirely without goals. It is safe to say that very rarely does anything get accomplished without a goal.

A person can be born into a wealthy family and be rich from the day they are born to the day they die without earning a dime themselves. That money, however, was earned and envisioned by the previous generation or even the generation before that. While in many cases a goal may be a certain weight or income, which is a great way to use goals, in other cases, we can think of and dream of a goal that will save our lives.

I told the story before of my teacher who took me under his wing and made me his water boy. By doing so, he helped me see a life outside of the devastation that was my reality. That was also the time when the football coach made a deal with the school that if I had perfect behavior, then I could play football. Then one of the football coaches I had gave me a flyer for a football camp at a university nearby. This was followed by a nice conversation with a scout at that football camp. Once I heard that I had the potential to possibly go to college to play football, I was over the moon. At this point in my life, I was in an alternative school and had very poor grades. It took

---

8   Earl Nightingale and Robert C. Worstell, *How to Change Your Life in 30 Seconds – Compleat* (Midwest Journal Press, 2017), 8.

all I could do to not get suspended, let alone excel enough to get into college. College was something I had not even considered. It was something that was out there or for other people. Once these people planted this seed of hope in my heart, I had a dream that was bigger than my problems or my past mistakes. This goal became my obsession, and it propelled me down a trail that I would never have known existed otherwise.

This goal was so huge in my life because it changed how I viewed so many things. I went from trying to not get in trouble at school to actually caring about it. I had a reason to get decent grades, whereas before school was just about survival. A good goal gives you a reason to do things that you might not want to do. A good goal can help you see past your current situation. The vision for what you long for can propel you with newfound passion. A good goal is a key part of any personal revolution. It can be a vision of a life that is different and a peek into a life worth leaving everything behind

GOALS THAT TORTURE YOU

While good goals have the power to save and change our lives, it is also possible that a lack of goals or failure to chase them can torture us. There is a price to be paid if we fail to take ownership. Have you ever set a goal for something and then lost track of it? Of course you have; we all have. We are all on a journey toward continuous improvement.

We have talked about the importance of goals, and I gave you a few examples from my life that have hopefully gotten you thinking about how they relate to your life. But one aspect of goal setting that can be painful and make you miserable is never setting any goals or doing nothing after you have set them.

Last year I set some goals for my weight. I gave myself a timeline to reach my goal about the same time that I would go on a family vacation. For a period of time, I went all out toward that goal and made some good progress. But life happened; I got distracted and failed to reach these goals I had set. Can you think of a time when that happened to you?

When the time came for this vacation, the goal I had set and the fact that I chose not to chase it down came to my mind many times. I chose to let my goal go and not make it mandatory. While I did enjoy my vacation, my goal that went unchased and unreached did put a damper on things. I kept thinking about how much more I would have enjoyed my free time had I reached that goal.

This is a small example of the pain of not chasing the goals we have. There can also be very big penalties for not setting goals and chasing them down. For example, you might set a goal to save for retirement but never get around to setting the funds aside. As time goes on, you miss out on all that compounding interest, and rather than lose a little money for a long time and retire with comfort, you get to retirement age and don't have enough money to retire. Therefore, rather than traveling and working in your garden, you are forced to get another job to supplement what little savings you have. This goal not chased will kick you in the gut pretty hard, and the regret will follow you.

Another example might be setting a goal to spend more time with aging parents or grandparents. You know they would love it and so would you, but you are busy and have your own family. Rather than going to see your parents, you do other things. These other things are important as well, no doubt, but regardless, these decisions are made because you figure that you can always catch up with them at another time. Then you are at a funeral, and while you sit there and listen to people talk about what a great person the deceased was, you think to yourself how you would have given up the other things that got in the way just to spend another afternoon with this person who is now gone. This goal not reached will haunt you forever because you will always regret doing other things and not taking the time.

As a last example, you might set a goal to get a degree and work in your desired field—the field you know you are built to work in. This goal would take schooling and discipline, but you know it is worth it. You know it is what you want to do with your life. When you get to college, you make some choices; you go out a few too many times and miss a few too many classes. Next thing you know, taking a semester off to save money sounds like a good idea. While you're off for that semester, a new car also sounds like a good idea. Your friends have new cars, so you say *you only live once*, and you buy one. Then twenty years have gone by; you have a family and are making a fraction of what you would be had you chased down that goal. As you work on a weekend or work all that overtime, you ride home from work and think to yourself *is this what I want from my life?* The pain and frustration overtake you, and it all comes crashing down as you think that you are wasting your life. That is by no means saying you are wasting your life; but this unrealized goal still haunts you.

The thought process behind bringing these issues up is not to call you out on things you did not do or to make you feel bad if one of those situations accurately describes your life. The idea is that life will go by either way. We want to be able to look back at our time and be happy with the choices we made—not swimming in a sea of regret.

YOUR GOAL WILL BE TESTED

When we step out and decide to make big changes in our lives, there will be times when other people will not be happy. In many cases, people will view your change as a threat. Your personal revolution can make them feel guilty for not making similar changes themselves. In some cases, they will simply not help you, and in others they will deliberately attempt to sabotage your growth. During the season of my life in which I underwent my personal revolution, I dealt with many people who were not happy that I was dreaming big.

The first big test came on the bus ride home shortly after my revolution chat with the high school football coach. I had a friend at the school who I had spent a great amount of time with in school as well as out of it. His name was Tim. Tim lived at home with his mom and stepdad. He had a very short fuse and would often just flip out on people, but up to this point, he had never flipped out on me. By flipping out, I mean that he would start screaming and swearing, and often his episodes would turn violent.

On the bus ride home, Tim started in on me for some reason. The bus was actually a van, and on this particular day I was in the seat in front of him. We had always been friends, so I was a little taken aback by Tim starting to pester me with comments like *you think you're better than everybody; you ain't nothing*. I did my best to ignore him, but he kept running his mouth. I just asked him to leave me alone. I didn't want any trouble. His response was that I wasn't looking for trouble, but it was looking for me, and then he blasted me in the back of the head with a punch. This all happened while we were riding down the road in the bus. The driver was an older woman, and she immediately pulled over as Tim continued to pound the back of my head. Of course, by this point, I had covered my head with my arms and scrunched down in the seat, so he was leaning over the seat in front of him and raining down blows.

The bus driver stopped the bus and came back to attempt to stop Tim, but he blasted her in the face with a punch. I then helped the bus driver shove him into the back seat, and she said she would call the cops. He started to calm down, so I moved to sit in the front of the van, and he sat in the back. All the while, he had occasional outbursts of screaming at me, but the bus driver was in the seat with him and was able to keep him back there. It didn't take long for another van to come pick me up and take me home.

Tim was a friend that turned on me like a light switch. I wanted to drive his head through a window with my fist. I wanted to punch him so hard and so bad that I daydreamed doing so on the rest of the van ride home. But I could not do it; I just kept thinking I couldn't do it because it would cost me too much.

If this fight had happened to me before my talk with the football coach, I have zero doubt that I would have attacked Tim back, and given the rage he brought out within me, I am not sure I would have ever stopped hitting him. But I chose not to because I had something I wanted more than to pulverize this bonehead. I wanted out; I wanted change, and Tim was not going to stand in my way.

A good goal will not only make you do things you may not want to, such as study hard or workout more, but also prevent you from doing things you may deeply want to do but can't because they don't fall in line with your goals.

To say this was the only challenge to my revolution would be silly; I had several. To say I was perfect after this trial would also be just as silly. I made mistakes along the way but none near the magnitude of the ones I had made prior to setting my goal.

- -ANSWER THESE QUESTIONS

Take a moment and think about your own life. Think about the challenges that are driving you crazy.

What are some of these challenges?

_____

_____

How are they driving you crazy?

_____

_____

Think about the goals you have or should have at this point in your life. What are some of the goals you have right now?

_____

_____

If you don't have any what goals, do you now see any goals that you should have right now?

_____

_____

Think on those questions for a moment.

Now think about you winning that game, getting that job, or reaching that goal. Let yourself go to that moment, and let yourself be there. Can you feel your heart filling with joy? As you imagine reaching that milestone, you can feel the freedom flow over your body and your heart leap with joy as you know it was a big goal, but you did it.

- -

A good goal is one that, when you think about it, fills your heart with joy and excitement. If your goal does not do this for you, it may not be big enough or personal enough for you to chase.

This is just one example of how a goal can change or save your life. Now we will dig into why and how we set goals.

CHAPTER TWELVE
How to Set a Goal

When we are thinking about goals and their role in our personal revolution, it is important to look at how to effectively set goals. There is a system to it that will help make them more reachable and increase our likelihood of enjoying the ride. Enjoying the ride is also a key factor in us actually finishing our goals.

For the sake of example, let's imagine you are a freshman in high school and want to be a lawyer. That is the destination; that is where you want to go. I hate to be the one to tell you this, but you will not wake up one day and magically be a lawyer. A good goal without a great plan is nothing more than a wish.

You want to be a lawyer; well to do that, you have to go to law school. To go to law school, you have to perform well in college. To perform well in college you have to first get in to a good college. To get in to a good college, you have to perform well in high school. To perform well in high school, you have to pass all your classes with high marks. To do that, you must pay attention in class and put the work in outside of the classroom. This includes the class you are sitting in as you think about being that lawyer. By taking the long-term goal of becoming a lawyer and working your way backward until you get to where you are right now, you put new value in the work you are doing today.

The goal of becoming a lawyer is a huge goal that has roadblocks and obstacles all along the way. Just thinking about such a large goal can be discouraging and make a person not even want to start; however, once you break the goal down and put a timeline to each task, you create hundreds of smaller goals along the way. As you put in the work and these smaller goals are reached, you will feel the momentum build. You know that you will not be a lawyer tomorrow, but you know that you will be closer to being one tomorrow than you are today. Big goals are great, but they must be broken down into smaller goals. This turns a goal that is huge and menacing into a reachable destination.

YOUR GOAL

While it is important for us to know how to set a great goal, it is even more important that the goals we set are our goals for our lives—not the goals of another person for our lives. If you do not take ownership of your goal and your life, you will be like a ship without a rudder that wanders aimlessly in hope of finding a harbor but is more likely to run up on the rocks. Your goal will require work, determination, planning, and execution. This is why it is so essential that it is *your* goal.

Let's jump back to our lawyer example and pretend mom and dad want you to be a lawyer, but you love the idea of helping people in other ways. You feel in your gut that being a doctor would be a fun way to earn a living. But because you feel pressure to be a lawyer because that is what others expect from you, you go to work chasing their dream for your life. This road involves the same school expectations, the same work, and the same time, but it is like climbing a ladder that is leaning against the wrong building. The goal is not what you want, and you climb and climb, all the while knowing it is not what you want for your life. Are you as likely to reach the goal? When the going gets tough and you have exams, work, and friends to balance, are you likely to make the right decisions? Are you more likely to spend an extra hour playing video games or an extra hour hitting the books? The idea is that if the goal is someone else's dream for you, following through will be that much more difficult. You might get halfway through school and decide that being a lawyer is not for you and give up. Now what? Now you have not finished anything, and this burden will lead to a truckload of regret.

Do you want to spend your days thinking *I should have been a doctor*? When you go to see a doctor, the thought that you could have done that will haunt you. Trace this moment back to that moment in high school when you chose to go someone else's direction instead of your own.

Life is full of people telling us what we should be doing with our lives. This does not stop when we get out of college. From our parents and other helpful family members to our boss, people will always be telling us what we should do. We have to listen to them to a point because in many cases they may be helping us and in most cases have good intentions. The trick to this is knowing what you want and owning it. If you fail to have a plan, plenty of people will come along and tell you what you should do. Do you want your destination or a destination set for you by others?

SET YOUR GOALS

Now is time for action. Not at a time down the road when all the lights turns green; all the lights will never be green. There will always be some obstacle or excuse not to decide what you want from life. Now we will do an exercise that outlines how to set a goal as well as some very common traps we all fall into when working on these goals.

ANSWER THESE QUESTIONS

As mentioned before, your goal must fill your heart with joy. It must be that thing that makes you so happy just to think about it. It must not be a silly goal like winning the lottery; surely that would make you happy, but what is it that you really want? Is it financial peace? Is it a degree in a certain field? Is it a family that you can love and serve? What do you want in life? These are not small questions; I challenge you to get a sheet of paper and start brainstorming things in your life that you want to change or progress you want to make.

What are some of your current goals?

_____

_____

How do you want to earn a living?

_____

_____

If you are having a hard time thinking of it, pretend you had all the money you could want. What would you do on Monday morning? What jobs would allow you to do that?

_____

_____

Where would you like to live? Why specifically would you want to live there?

_____

_____

Do you want a family? What about having a family fills your heart with joy?

_____

_____

Do you have fitness goals, like to do a 5k or a marathon?

_____

_____

What hobbies look fun to you that you would love to take up—horseback riding, flying lessons, motorcycle riding?

_____

_____

- -

STEPS IN THE GOAL SETTING PROCESS

Step 1: Write it Down

Writing down a goal is the first step in taking it from a simple wish to a goal. If you write it down, you make a contract with yourself. You make a commitment to yourself that you are going to go all in on this and make it happen. There is something about writing important things down. Once you have your goals written down, put some sticky notes in places to keep your goals in the front of your mind. For example, if you have a specific goal for your performance at work, put a sticky note near your speedometer on your car. Each day on your way to work, you put your mind in the right place. If your goal is a health goal, maybe put a sticky note on your refrigerator. Put these dreams to paper and put them in front of you so you can stay on track. While you will still have bad days, you will certainly get further by writing your goal down and focusing on it consistently rather than just thinking of it one day and then forgetting about it.

Step 2: Make a Plan

Once you have set some goals and written them down, you want to start planning for your goals. For example, if you want to write a book, plan out when you will set aside time to work on it. What days of the week will you go off by yourself and work on it? Where will you get new ideas from, and what books will you read to prepare yourself for this project? Planning out a goal is similar to putting your destination into the GPS; you put it in and hit Go. Once you hit Go, you can see the roads you need to take and an approximate time at which you will reach your destination. If you put your destination in but never hit Go, the destination will be viewable on the screen, but you will have no clue which roads to take.

A great way to make your plan is to look at others who have reached similar goals. Think back to the role models you have and determine whether there are people in your life that can help you with this plan. If you don't personally know anyone who has reached those goals, maybe look outside of your circle of friends. For example, if you want to be an actor and are not sure where to start, find some people who are doing it well and follow their path. With Wikipedia, you don't even need people to have written biographies to do this kind of research. Find someone else's path and adjust their plan to fit your life. Then get moving.

Step 3: Set a Timeline

An idea with a date is a goal; an idea with no date is a wish. We have all had ideas that, when we look back on them, we think *why didn't I do that?* The reason is that we never wrote it down, made a plan, or gave ourselves a deadline. In school, business, and virtually every significant project there are deadlines. They are there for a reason. They are a tool to ensure completion. They are there to help drive the progress. When life is busy, we will use these deadlines to keep us on track. This is the difference between a goal reached and a wish not granted.

Step 4: Make it Mandatory

Once you have searched your heart and found some goals that fire you up, written them down, made a plan, and set a timeline, then is the time to make them mandatory. Making a goal mandatory is the opposite of making it optional. This is an adjustment in our mindset that totally changes how we view and pursue our goals. Things that are optional often get set aside for things that are mandatory. If you set the right goal, then it should be very important to you. Pursuing it is not optional but mandatory. Life will give us all kinds of distractions and excuses to put our goals down, but our mindset toward that goal will be the difference. For example, if you set a goal to be debt free, which is a great goal, but let it be optional, you leave all kinds of room for discretionary mistakes. If you set this goal and it is mandatory, you know that when you go to the mall, you cannot buy those shoes on your credit card. There might be a great sale that is ending soon, and an optional goal would result in using your credit card to buy the shoes. If it is a mandatory goal, the decision has been made; either you pay cash or don't buy them. If you have the cash, buy them. If you don't, you can't. Making the goal mandatory gives it more power, and it gives us more power to walk away from failure.

ROADBLOCKS

To say that by writing a goal down, planning it out, and giving it a date, you will just magically get to where you want to be is silly. You will encounter roadblocks. If there were no roadblocks, there would be no challenge to goals, meaning those goals are most likely not big enough. But if you think about the potential roadblocks ahead of time, you can get your mind in the right place before you run into them. Knowing about the roadblocks will allow you to not only prepare for them but also avoid many of them. A great example of this would be a traffic app that alerts you to construction, accidents, and even the police. If you are on a big trip and the app tells you that traffic is backing up near a large city, you can adjust your route to avoid the traffic. Knowing of these roadblocks ahead of time helps us make better choices on our trip. Looking ahead in our goal-chasing process is just the same. It will still be a challenge, but it will be much easier if we know where the roadblocks are. Some we can steer clear of and others we can navigate better knowing that they are part of the process. We will dive into a couple of the many roadblocks that we may have in our path.

Weight loss is the biggest New Year's resolution. At the beginning of every new year, people say they are going to lose that extra weight. They start off eating healthy and going to the gym on January first. Try going to the gym at the beginning of January and then go at the same time at the end of January or beginning of February. It is full at the beginning and as time goes by, the rush to win the resolution has faded.

What happened to all of these gym rats? What happens to all of us at times is that we miss a key aspect of goal reaching. We eat healthy and go to the gym and then one day you go to company party and they have pizza. You eat some, and this is the first time you have cheated since you started losing weight. Then later on, when you get home, you think to yourself that since you had pizza today already, you must have blown it and might as well have some cookies before bed. Then you wake up the next day and think that since yesterday you had pizza and cookies, you might as well have pancakes instead of yogurt for breakfast.

This sounds funny on paper, but look at your life and the goals you have set in the past; if you are like most people, you will find that the day after failure is very important. To think you will go on with your goal and never fail is silly. You will make mistakes, but a goal is bigger than one mistake. For a ship that is going to cross the sea, from a bird's eye view, the path is a straight line across the ocean. If you examine the ship close up and see its exact navigation, you will find that the path has ebbs and flows. There are gusts of wind, large waves, and inclement weather that will push the ship from side to side. The captain has to constantly put the ship back on course to ensure a safe arrival. So it goes with our goals; we will have waves of apparent failure, but we just correct our course and move on. Knowing that minor failures will happen going into the journey makes the failures feel like part of the ride, not the end of it.

Roadblock 2: Goals Change

One of the biggest roadblocks we face when chasing a dream or a goal is that we at times have to change them. This is not like gusts of wind blowing our ship temporarily off course; this is the ship sinking. This happens to us often in life. As we work toward something, we come to the conclusion that something we thought was for us may not be. For example, you may set a goal to work your way up the ladder at a company and then the company has massive financial concerns and lays you off or goes out of business. This is a common pitfall for many people. First know that these things happen and that at times there is nothing you can do about it. But before you drown in the sea of regret and depression about failing yet again, think about your situation from another perspective.

Our ability to be happy in life is determined by our ability to deal with change in the appropriate manner.

This is a lesson that I had to learn the hard way. I wrote earlier about how the goal I had to play college football saved my life. I also started off the book talking about the massive depression and obesity I had in the middle of my college life. When I got to college and was on the football team, I sustained some injuries that prevented me from continuing with my dream. I had to have surgery on both of my feet and was advised to walk away from football. This was such a low point for me because I had worked so hard on this dream. I had placed my whole identity in this dream and felt that because I had failed to reach this goal, I was a failure.

What I did not realize at the time was that the dream still saved my life. While I never played a down of college football, the dream of doing so propelled me to go to college. It not only inspired me to change my life but also gave me a roadmap to do so. When this dream died, it hurt all the way to my soul, but after some time of throwing a pity party for myself, I came to the conclusion that while the dream did not come true, I was better off for having set it.

The destinations will change at times, and as people, we will face roadblocks. But we must view our work toward reaching that goal, though the goal may change, as something that still made us better.

While the bridge of the train tracks that lead toward your goal may get blown up, you must remember that you are still better off for having set that goal. Using the example before about working your way up in your company, you might remember that you worked hard and gave your best. Your goal drove you to learn new things, step outside of your comfort zone, and challenge yourself to get better. These are all things another company will cherish and can be added to your resume. If you had not worked that hard and not learned new things, another company might view you as a nester who doesn't want to grow. The idea is that while you may not have reached the goal you set, you are still better off for having chased it.

Our ability to enjoy our lives is riding on our ability to know what we want to do with our lives and strive to get there. If you don't own your life and your goals, someone or something else will. Life happens to all of us, and we can't go back and rewind. We must set a course in our ship of life. If we just set sail, we will surely go nowhere. Take inventory of what you really want, and go get it. The ship is going to sea no matter what; it is up to us to decide which port it is headed to. Goals have the ability to give us all we want in life, but like most things, we must learn how to use them properly. To this point, we have covered several large topics to help you start a personal revolution. We have looked at self-image, attitude, the role of others, and goals. What we do now as the picture gets clearer is we see how they are all connected.

To get where we want to go we must have a goal. To have a goal, we have to surround ourselves with people who see the best in us. To know who the people are that see the best in us, we must first have a positive attitude toward the people in our lives. To have a positive attitude toward the people in our lives, we must first learn to see the best in ourselves.

This is a simple, logical, and realistic way to look at our lives. A personal revolution is much like this path. Start with how you see yourself, then how you see your world, then how you see those around you, and lastly where you want to go. While it is tempting, you can't skip a step. If you try to set goals without a proper understanding of your self-esteem, you will most likely end up chasing someone else's goal. If you try to fix your attitude without involving others who will be honest with you, you will end up thinking you have it all figured out while the people around you may not agree.

– –ANSWER THESE QUESTIONS

When you talk to yourself, what are you saying?

_____

_____

What tone are you using?

_____

_____

When you see your world, do you see it as being good to you?

_____

Did you grasp the fact that you create your world by how you see it?

_____

Who in your life is living how you want to live?

_____

Who in your life can help you get where you want to go?

_____

Who in your life can you help get where they want to go?

_____

What is your destination?

_____

How do you see yourself earning a living?

_____

What idea or ideal keeps you up at night with excitement as you imagine achieving it?

_____

What are some of the things still in your way?

_____

We will finish purging these last roadblocks in the final chapter.

- -

CHAPTER THIRTEEN
Personal Revolution

It has been said that life is a journey. This makes sense because we are moving along a path as we grow up. As time goes by, we reach new milestones, much like we do as we drive across the country on a road trip. If this is the case, then the goal of life is to get to the end of it. But that is not the goal of life; the goal of life is to live it!

Think about a time when you went to a movie that you were looking forward to seeing for months. You don't go to the theater, check the length of the movie, set a timer on your phone, and look forward to the end. You go in with excitement, enthusiasm, and anticipation as you get your popcorn and make your way to your seat. The lights go down, and you take in all the previews. You see previews for several new movies that you think look amazing.

Then the movie starts. It has your favorite actor playing your favorite character. During the course of this adventure, your hero on the screen runs into a problem, and it looks like he is doomed. He works his way though, and usually by the hair of his chin, he defeats the bad guys and often wins the girl.

Throughout the movie, you took it in, enjoyed the plot, and were excited about the experience. You were not waiting for the end; as a matter of fact, you were bummed when it ended. If life is lived like a journey, we look forward to the end. We check our phones and wonder when the movie is over while the amazing story is going on in front of us on the giant screen. It does not take much to see that waiting for the movie to be over without enjoying it is truly wasting it. It is wasting all the time it took to make the movie, all the great stories it told, and most of all, our time.

Your personal revolution is about making sure you don't waste any more of your life from this day forward. That is not to say you have wasted your life to this point, but if you have read this far into the book, you are looking for something more, and that is what a personal revolution is about. It is about letting go of the old, outdated issues you are struggling with and embracing the amazing future you have.

Personal revolution is taking the old-as-time concepts, such as self-image and attitude, and actually buying into them. Once you truly understand that they are real ideas that work in real life, they can help you find freedom. You are bound and are looking for freedom, and when you find it, you are filled with energy and passion. This energy and passion is the revolution. You learn to look at work as fun, and you learn to look at the future with excitement. The same tasks that in the past were all work are now part of the journey.

Through the trip we took in this book, we have unpacked many life-changing concepts that, if properly applied, will lead you to a much better life. We will now launch into a final exercise to ensure your revolution gets started with a clean slate.

FINAL EXERCISE

If you have been bound by the chains we have been working to break in this book, today is the day that you break free. If you have had a low self-image up until this point in your life and want to break free, today is your day. If a bad attitude is something you have been battling with off and on throughout your whole life, today is the day you choose to win that battle. If you have dealt with bullies or domestic violence and this has you feeling like you are locked in a cell, today you kick down the door! If you have thought the world would be better without you in it, today you throw that lie in the trash. The final exercise of this book will require you to get yourself off the sidelines and into the game. The coach just called your number. Your future is counting on you, and you will never be the same.

What Is the Next Step?

There was a couple that enjoyed going to the circus. One time when they went to the circus, they went to the offstage area where all the animals were being kept. They enjoyed the circus, but seeing all the animals was by far their favorite part. They really were mesmerized by the elephant. It was such a big, amazing animal yet graceful, and it just struck a chord with the couple.

As the couple went backstage to see the elephant, they couldn't help but notice that the elephant was being held by a small, single rope. At the end of this rope was a small stake. It seemed very odd that the elephant, with all of its amazing power, was being held captive by a small, harmless rope and a stake not much larger than one used on a tent.

Curiosity overcame this couple, and they were determined to find out how this could be. They sought out and found one of the elephant's trainers and asked them how such a large, powerful, and smart animal could be held by such meager restraints.

The trainer explained to the couple the story behind the rope and the stake. When an elephant is born into captivity, it is removed from its mother straight away. It is not given more than the essential nutrients to survive but is taken and has this rope tied around its leg.

The baby elephant tugs and tugs on the rope, but it is held captive by a very large anchor. For a day, sometimes two, the elephant tugs and screams as it tries to get loose from the anchor that is holding it. After a short time, the baby elephant gives up and accepts the fact that it can not gain its freedom.

After a day or so, the baby elephant, having given up on pulling away from the rope, is taken by the trainers and put back with its mother. The rope is kept on its leg at all times. The elephant goes through its life with this rope on its leg and never tries to break free because it knows that the rope is too strong and the anchor is too heavy for the elephant to ever break free of.

As time goes on, this elephant grows large enough to crush a car or walk through the walls of a house, but it does not realize its own strength. It simply remembers that the rope is holding it in place. It is held captive by the *memory* of the strength of the rope. The rope no longer has any legitimate power over the elephant, but the memory of the rope keeps it captive.

- **ANSWER THESE QUESTIONS**

What are the ropes in your life?

_____

_____

What is the tiny stake that is holding you captive?

_____

_____

What memories are keeping you roped to a stake?

_____

_____

- -

Now is the time for you to take serious, legitimate action and investigate the rope around your leg. This exercise requires you to get a piece of paper.

Now that you have your paper and a pen, ponder these questions.

When you talk to yourself what are you saying? Is it negative and self-defeating? Write down on this piece of paper all of the negative things you say to yourself: "I am too fat, tall, short, white, black, old, or poor." Get it all out. Take a few moments and jot all of these thoughts down.

When you see your world, what do you see? Do you see a negative future filled with fear and failure? Write down all of the negative things you think about when you view your world. Take a few moments and get them all on the paper.

Think about all the people in your past that have hurt you—the parents who maybe weren't there, the bully who made you feel small, the boss who made you hate your job. Think hard on this one. Write down all of the people who hurt you and offended you, in the past as well as currently.

Lastly think about all of your big mistakes that keep you up at night. Think about the relationships you destroyed with unkind words or actions or the time you blew up at a loved one and made it so the relationship has never been the same. Get those mistakes all on the paper. You may need another sheet of paper. Put everything about your past that is haunting you on the paper.

Please pause for just a moment and read everything on your sheet(s) of paper. As you read them, maybe more people or thoughts or memories come to mind. That is okay; write them down too. This is the part of your personal revolution where you *do* something that unpacks all this junk and puts it down on paper.

Now that you have this all-inclusive sheet of paper of all the mean, nasty things in your life, the things that are haunting you, and the things that are standing in your way, think about that baby elephant. What you have right now in front of you is your rope tied to a tent stake. There was a time that these things did bind you, but that time is gone. The memories off all of these things are holding you captive, like a small rope and a tent stake.

The next thing you need to do is get a small pot from the kitchen, get some matches, and head outside.

As you stand in your driveway or on your deck read, the paper one last time. Think of all the pain and suffering and frustration those pages contain. Do a symbolic act, and tear that sheet of paper to shreds. If you have thought this through, while you are tearing it up, you will feel a wave of emotion as you let these things go. As you rip, rip, rip the paper into shreds, you are taking the power from these issues and removing the rope from your leg.

Now take all of this shredded paper and place it in the pot. As you look down at it one last time, think about the freedom that lies ahead of you. Think of the great things you will say to yourself from now on. Think of the forgiveness you have given to all those who have hurt you.

With joy, confidence, and freedom, light the paper on fire and watch it burn. As you are watching it burn, think of yourself as that giant elephant with the rope no longer around its leg. You are now crushing the small, tiny stake. This is an action, but it is an act of faith that you are going to start your revolution right now and never look back.

Down the road, as new things come up that remind you of what was in that pot in your driveway, just remember that you burned it up. You have removed the rope, crushed the stake, and are now free to get on with enjoying your life.

Personal revolution is just that—personal. The stories I shared from my life were only tools to lead you to this moment where you could declare yourself free.

Walk in this freedom, friends, and never look back.

About the Author

Joshua Spears has been sharing his story and speaking to school audiences since 2002.

He shares his passion for life with students as he works to drive change in the lives of others. Joshua grew up in a very volatile home riddled with domestic violence and dysfunction, but because of the work of many dedicated teachers and family members, he was able to turn his life around. He began speaking to schools immediately after graduating from college.

Joshua has held many management positions throughout his career but kept coming back to his passion—helping people. He has a strong passion for helping people find their value, the value of others, and the value of their future.

In his free time, Joshua enjoys reading, volunteering, and working in the yard. But his favorite thing to do is spend time with his amazing wife, Julie, and their three boys, Charlie, Danny, and Benji.

APPENDIX
Suggested Books to Read

* *As a Man Thinketh* by James Alan

* *7 Habits of Highly Effective People* by Steven Covey

* *The Strangest Secret* by Earl Nightingale

* *Self-Reliance* by Ralph Waldo Emerson

* *Motivation Manifesto* by Brendon Burchard

* *Finish* by Jon Acuff

* *Failing Forward* by John Maxwell

Bibliography

1.   Allen, James. *As a Man Thinketh*. Longmeadow Press, 2009.

2.   "Definition of Revolution." Merriam-Webster. September 19, 2018. https://www.merriam-webster.com/dictionary/revolution.

3.   Liker, Jeffrey K. *The Toyota Way*. McGraw Hill, 2004.

4.   Maxwell, John C. *15 Invaluable Laws of Growth*. Hachette Book Group, 2012.

5.   Nightingale, Earl and Robert C. Worstell, *How to Change Your Life in 30 Seconds – Compleat*. Midwest Journal Press, 2017.

www.ingramcontent.com/pod-product-compliance
Lightning Source LLC
Chambersburg PA
CBHW060400050426
42449CB00009B/1830